Improving
Student Learning

Also available from ASQ Quality Press

The New Philosophy for K–12 Education: A Deming Framework for Transforming America's Schools
James F. Leonard

Orchestrating Learning with Quality
David P. Langford and Barbara A. Cleary, Ph.D.

Kidgets: And Other Insightful Stories About Quality in Education
Maury Cotter and Daniel Seymour

Total Quality for Schools: A Guide for Implementation
Joseph C. Fields

The Quality Toolbox
Nancy R. Tague

Mapping Work Processes
Dianne Galloway

Team Fitness: A How-To Manual for Building a Winning Work Team
Meg Hartzler and Jane E. Henry, Ph.D.

The Change Agents' Handbook: A Survival Guide for Quality Improvement Champions
David W. Hutton

Quality Quotes
Hélio Gomes

To request a complimentary catalog of publications, call 800-248-1946.

Improving Student Learning

Applying Deming's Quality Principles in Classrooms

Lee Jenkins

ASQ Quality Press
Milwaukee, Wisconsin

Improving Student Learning: Applying Deming's Quality Principles in Classrooms
Lee Jenkins

Library of Congress Cataloging-in-Publication Data
Jenkins, Lee.
    Improving student learning: applying Deming's quality principles
in classrooms / Lee Jenkins.
        p.   cm.
    Includes bibliographical references and index.
    ISBN 0-87389-410-3 (alk. paper)
    1. School improvement programs—United States.   2. Learning.
3. Total quality management—United States.   4. Deming, W. Edwards
(William Edwards), 1900–1993.   5. Educational tests and measurements—
United States.   I. Title.
LB2822.82.J46   1997
371.2'00973—dc20

                                        96-34154
                                        CIP

© 1997 by ASQ

10 9 8 7 6 5 4

ISBN 0-87389-410-3

Acquisitions Editor: Kelley Cardinal
Project Editor: Kelley Cardinal

ASQ Mission: To facilitate continuous improvement and increase customer satisfaction by identifying, communicating, and promoting the use of quality principles, concepts, and technologies; and thereby be recognized throughout the world as the leading authority on, and champion for, quality.

Attention: Schools and Corporations
ASQ Quality Press books, audiotapes, videotapes, and software are available at quantity discounts with bulk purchases for business, educational, or instructional use. For information, please contact ASQ Quality Press at 800-248-1946, or write to ASQ Quality Press, P.O. Box 3005, Milwaukee, WI 53201-3005.

For a free copy of the ASQ Quality Press Publications Catalog, including ASQ membership information, call 800-248-1946.

Printed in the United States of America

  Printed on acid-free paper

American Society for Quality

ASQ™

Quality Press
611 East Wisconsin Avenue
P.O. Box 3005
Milwaukee, Wisconsin 53201-3005

This book is dedicated to
Rev. Kenneth L. Jenkins, my father

Somewhere in my teens I asked, "Dad, if you moved to a new church wouldn't you have it real easy? You could re-preach all the same sermons and wouldn't have to work so hard." He responded, "It doesn't work that way, because all your life you grow and develop. The sermons of a couple years ago just aren't good enough today." My appreciation for quality and continuous improvement started young and is due, to a large extent, to this wonderful man who lives all week the sermons he preaches on Sunday.

CONTENTS

FIGURES AND TABLES

Figures

Tables

FOREWORD

As this book clearly demonstrates, the Enterprise School District is aptly named: Its teachers and administrators are truly enterprising in their use of innovative learning strategies. If quality is a journey—and it surely is—then this book moves us a very long way along the journey toward having schools that are continuously improving through the use of quality concepts and techniques.

We were fortunate enough to have studied with W. Edwards Deming for several years—a significant educational event in our lives—during the period when he was especially interested in American education. As students and practitioners of Dr. Deming's concepts, we have worked for the past five years to introduce his concepts in schools. It is a difficult endeavor, as educators are wary of innovations that promise great improvement, especially when those innovations come from the business sector. Under the inspiring leadership of Lee Jenkins, the concepts come to life in classrooms and school buildings.

With this book, Dr. Jenkins has captured the excitement and power that develops when quality comes to the classroom. This can be seen in the many examples of how quality tools are used by learners, both students and teachers—examples that are clear, meaningful, and significant. The way in which the author uses creative analogies helps readers understand the concepts and feel confident using quality tools. The classroom application of the tools is a real contribution to the quality emphasis.

Dr. Jenkins remains true to the Deming approach in explaining the quality ideas and concepts, effectively translating Deming's techniques for the education world. The discussion of *system* is one of the best, simplest, most coherent explanations we have seen of this important concept. Likewise, the chapter on psychology, another element of profound knowledge, is clear and easy to apply.

This book is marked by a sound, commonsense approach to applying new concepts and techniques to education. It is clear that the author is, first and foremost, an educator—and a very good one, at that. He is an educator who understands the quality approach, not a quality practitioner who purports to understand education. This is an important distinction that explains why this book will be so useful for educators. They will immediately recognize the genuine and authentic nature of the examples and will be able to see the applications to their own situation. The charts and illustrations that demonstrate the use of data in the classroom are particularly valuable and provide a form of "grading" that can be much more meaningful and helpful to students and parents. The "smiley" charts show how a simple tool can be used effectively (and yet tell a devastating story).

Perhaps the most telling aspect of this book is that the author lays the responsibility for school change squarely at the feet of educational leaders. It is the leaders—boards, administrators, and teachers—who must provide the direction and strategies for school change. The Enterprise School District has done just that, using the concepts of total quality as a guide. The emphasis on process management, both in the classroom and in the district, is transforming education in the community.

Linda A. Borsum
Executive Vice President
IRI—Total Quality
    Learning Systems

Chester A. Francke, Ph.D.
General Director, Joint
    Education Activities
General Motors Corporation
    (retired)

Co-Chairs of the
1997 National Governors' Conference
on Education and Quality

PREFACE

This book is about improving student learning; it is written for teachers and others who have a passion for teaching and learning. The classroom is center stage.

Improvement occurs because somebody's theory is proven accurate. All innovation is first in the mind before it is created in actuality. Thus, improved learning occurs because a teacher has a theory in his or her head, tries out the theory, and notes that student learning has improved.

If an educational theory does not improve classroom learning it matters not how many legislators, editors, or other leaders ascribe to the theory; it is useless.

The management theory of Dr. W. Edwards Deming improves student learning. Some may ask, "Didn't he advise manufacturers? What does that have to do with teaching school?" Dr. Deming advised owners of manufacturing firms on how to *better manage their people* to create an improved manufactured product. He gave the same advice to educators on how to *better manage their people* to create improved learning. It matters not that a person is managing 25 people producing brakes or 25 people producing better learning. It matters not that some people are tall and some are short. The theories of Dr. Deming are as powerful for teachers and their leaders as they are for businesses.

Most of *Improving Student Learning* is set in the classroom. How can teachers know if the changes made in instructional strategies really do result in improved learning? Can teachers document that this year's students are learning better than last year's students? Can parents and students clearly see growth themselves, or do they have to take somebody else's word that learning has taken place? Is there improved learning that parents and students can understand? Dr. Deming told leaders they have the responsibility to create joy in the workplace. How can educators know if they are maintaining the joy of learning contained inside their kindergartners?

Teachers are typically treated like members of a bowling team. Faculty members enter their own classrooms, teach as they see fit, and the scores are added up once each year. When teachers see the power of thinking about their students as a team working toward a common goal, they naturally desire to become a team member themselves. But, can teachers be treated like orchestra members rather than bowling team members? Yes they can, and so there's a chapter on schoolwide improvement. This chapter is not a treatise on how the principal can leverage more work from a staff, but how teachers can work together with their principal to create a powerful team. And what is the energy that fuels this orchestra of educators? It is improvement. People become addicted to the joy of knowing that their school is improving every year and to the understanding that, most likely, next year will be even better than this year.

One chapter is included on districtwide improvement. Why? Because teachers and principals want the team to include everyone. Again, this chapter is not about how the superintendent and school board can strategize to wring more effort from people, but how to maximize effort and talent. Much energy is wasted in every school district because one employee or school, in pursuit of an individual objective, is undoing the work of another employee or school. Districtwide improvement is not top-down, nor is it site based. It is *we* agreeing on an aim, having in-depth discussions on methods, and collecting the data to know when improvement has actually occurred.

Improving Student Learning includes more than 150 figures. Because education degrees often include never-used statistics and many have been taught by newspapers to see statistics as harmful, educators often wince at graphs and statistics. Dr. Deming would have educators replace useless and harmful statistics with useful, helpful statistics. The graphs in this book are simple and profound. One month before writing this preface a teacher showed me her graphs for the month of March. They documented that this year's class had already surpassed the end-of-year learning of prior years' classes. This type of data and joy have never before been available to teachers.

As you read *Improving Student Learning* I hope you capture the enthusiasm from each of the classrooms and understand that you, too, can improve the lives of your students with Dr. Deming's quality principles.

Lee Jenkins
ljenkins@enterprise.k12.ca.us

ACKNOWLEDGMENTS

One of Dr. Deming's admonitions was, "Learn from the masters; they are few." Long before I knew of Dr. Deming's work, I met one of these masters, Evelyn Neufeld. She taught first grade in Santa Clara, California, where I was assigned to teach fifth grade. For two wonderful years, I was able to watch her teach during my recesses and lunch. I asked her question after question about Piaget, mathematics, and learning. Evelyn set the standard. Over the next 30 years other masters crossed my career path and were proven to be equally talented.

Peggy McLean taught me that science could be as easily learned as mathematics. Mary Laycock mentored Peggy and me while she published our mathematical works. Mary is one of the few in the United States who can teach mathematics well from kindergarten through advanced college.

Because of Evelyn's, Peggy's, and Mary's mentoring I was hired by the Fullerton Schools as their coordinator of mathematics and science. The Fullerton bonus was Marion Nordberg, who tutored me for three years in the teaching of reading and writing. Even though she had 500 visitors a year to watch her teach she always had time for me to sit down and learn.

Bill Martin Jr., the children's author, was the next master. His explanations of how language works, his facility with the written word, and his care for children have greatly influenced my work as an educator. For more than 20 years he has caringly provided wisdom.

The next master I wish to acknowledge is Vic Cottrell, the Nebraska psychologist who has studied excellent educators for more than 30 years. Like the others I've acknowledged, I'll never learn all Vic has to offer regarding bringing out the best in others.

Without the influence of these six people, I would never have recognized the genius of Dr. Deming. Lew Rhodes, Judy Nash, and Martha Bozman of the American Association of School Administrators urged me to hear about quality and W. Edwards Deming in 1990. At their invitation I attended a wonderful seminar by Susan Leddick, who has continued her teaching, mentoring, and provocative question asking. Because the stage had been set by the aforementioned six, it was easy to recognize that Dr. Deming was a person who could provide the same quality of help in administration and leadership that I knew existed in other aspects of schooling.

Within the Enterprise School District are many individuals who assisted, encouraged, and carried out the details of improvement. They begin with the board president Gloria Valles, who has supported me in the quality journey every step of the way. B. J. Olson never knew when she accepted the position as superintendent's secretary that this meant competence in statistics, graphs, and graphics. Support and encouragement are her middle names. The administrators, Nancy Schultz, Bill Rich, Harry Morris, Cass Ditzler, Rick Fauss, Denny Mills, Bill Watkins, Jack Greenfield, Dana Reginato, Ken Harbord, Tom Armelino, Brian Winstead, and Sharon Stennett have each supported my efforts. They have internalized the improvement process for classrooms, schools, and the district as a whole.

Without teacher leadership, however, this book could not exist. It's the people who added to their overloaded responsibility list a new idea from their superintendent who deserve the most credit. Damon Cropsey and Arlene Oleari-Johnson did the very first run charts and scatter diagrams. Dan Flores provided significant new insights; Karen Fauss regularly showed me her students' improved learning; and Suzan Harvey explored new applications in mathematics. Lavon Altic and Pam Amador lead the reading improvement efforts described early in the book; Guy Piché led secondary experiments; and both Traci Wierman and Judy Flores devoted hours of their own time to mathematics improvement.

Finally, there's Sandy, my wife. She has encouraged and listened, always wondering what is coming next. She's friends with most of those mentioned in these acknowledgments, which shows her partnership in all that I do. Every superintendent should be so blessed.

INTRODUCTION

Education has undergone change after change accompanied by subsequent reversal to former practices. Continual changes must be replaced with improvement. Education can no longer afford expensive changes and the ensuing debates over the efficacy of each change.

The twentieth century had just begun. France had already failed; the United States was almost ready to call it quits. The problem was not money, talent, technology, or determination. It was dropouts. People were dropping out completely—six feet under.

The location was Panama; the challenge was the Panama Canal.[1] The problem: yellow fever. Up to 50 percent of each new shipload of workers died from yellow fever. Nobody knew the cause of yellow fever, but conventional wisdom was to blame the worker. People thought those who contracted yellow fever had a deficiency either in character or health habits. But blame did not eradicate yellow fever.

If blame could improve schooling, American K–12 education would be the envy of the world. Everybody is blaming everybody, but few are looking for root causes of educational problems. In the midst of the Panama yellow fever crisis, blaming seemed reasonable. Looking back, however, blaming seems quite silly. Yellow fever was built into the Panamanian system; it was not the fault of the workers. Ants in Panama were biting people in their sleep, so people placed dishes of water under each bedpost. The nightly ant bites stopped, but, of course, the mosquitoes spreading yellow fever had more breeding water. The solution to an irritant caused death.

It is hoped that America will be able to look back on the current crisis in K–12 education and laugh at the practice of blaming workers—administrators, teachers, students, and parents. Just like Panama, America will find that failure is not coming from the workers, but from the system. What is education's counterpart to the bedpost water bowls of Panama? Dr. W. Edwards Deming clearly identified the counterparts and solutions. First, however, is a look at blaming. What's wrong with blaming?

1. It *fixes nothing.* The legislature and press blame the education *establishment,* the school board blames the superintendent, the superintendent blames the principals, the principals blame the teachers, the teachers blame the parents, and nothing improves for the students.

2. Blaming lets *those in charge escape responsibility.* As long as blaming persists, everyone's job is to convince the boss that he or she is not the one responsible for the problem. For example, school cooks know that the person who buys the food, develops the menu, and sets cafeteria policies has the most control over the profit-loss statement for the food service program of the school district. But if cooks, who have no power to change the system, are blamed for a cafeteria loss, the situation continues with those in charge escaping responsibility. The food service supervisor has escaped responsibility by convincing the business manager that the cooks are at fault.

3. Blaming *stops the search for underlying causes.* Usually current problems are caused by yesterday's solutions to former problems. If nobody is looking for underlying causes, then today's problems are not being connected to yesterday's solutions. For example, suppose a middle school changes from a seven-period day to a six-period day to solve a school problem. Everything seems to be OK, except that band cannot fit into the six-period day and must be taught before school. That seems satisfactory to parents and students, but nobody wants students to arrive at school in the dark. So, the school starting time is moved ahead 20 minutes. This also seems fine, but now the bus system cannot handle the change and an elementary school has one bus that is late 20 minutes each day. The staff at the elementary school blames the transportation department for running an inefficient system, without knowing that the root cause of the problem is a decision to allow another school across town to alter its schedule. Today's bus problem is caused by yesterday's solution to an unpopular student schedule.

Improving Student Learning describes how to replace blaming and excuses with quality education.

Note

1. David McCullough, *The Path Between the Seas* (New York: Simon and Schuster, 1977).

Section I
Improvement Basics

Chapter 1
AN AIM FOR EDUCATION

Every system includes seven elements. An organization without each of the seven elements is a collection of parts, not a system. Brakes, engine, steering wheel, and transmission do not add up to a car that works. Likewise teachers, buildings, budget, and instructional materials do not add up to a school system that works. Crucial to the understanding of Dr. Deming is the understanding of *system*. Dr. Deming was fond of citing the following example. You could bring to one location the dozen best cars in the world. The top automotive experts in the world could determine which cars had the best engine, which had the best steering, which had the best brakes, and so on. These best parts could be collected from the best cars by the best experts, and what you would have is a collection of parts, but not one working automobile.

The automobile metaphor is crucial to understanding improvement. To have a working car, all the parts must be in place and they must work together. The seven components of a system are *aim, customers, suppliers, input, process, output,* and *quality measurement.* If any component is missing or not in tandem with the other six parts, one has a collection of pieces, but not a system. Looking at education, one would have to conclude that it is a collection of pieces, not a system. Unfortunately, a mediocre school with one world-class part is often considered an above-average school. Never mind that the parts are not working together as a system.

The first requirement for a system is to have an aim. Without an aim the parts will never work together as a system. Spelling instruction is an example of an aimless segment of education. Spelling instruction in the United States has perfected its process. The process is a Friday test. But how do students know if they have accomplished success in spelling? They don't know, because nobody told them the aim in spelling. The spelling test in week 1 generally has nothing to do with week 2 spelling or any other week's spelling. It is merely a collecting of Friday tests that, when added up, equal a collection of tests. So, the first step in improving spelling instruction in any school district is to establish an aim. An example of a spelling aim is for students to know how to spell, by a particular grade, the 1000 words most often used in English.

Dr. Deming offered the following overall aim for education: "Increase the positives and decrease the negatives so that all students keep their yearning for learning."[1] He knew that if students could only keep the enthusiasm for learning they had in kindergarten they could be successful in school. The aim of the educational system, for Dr. Deming, was to figure out which positives help students keep their joy and spread those positives to all classrooms. Conversely, educators must also determine the negatives that remove joy and eliminate those practices.

Moving away from education's collection of parts to Dr. Deming's quality system requires an aim. Other system statements, such as a mission, tenets, and vision, are all valuable for planning, but a precise, all-encompassing aim is essential to beginning the process of educational improvement. The mission, tenets, and vision are rings on the organizational target; the aim is the bull's-eye.

Note

1. W. Edwards Deming, American Association of School Administrators Conference, Washington, D.C., January 1992.

Chapter 2
IMPROVEMENT INSTEAD OF CHANGE

Education in the United States is at the same place the automobile industry was several years ago. Every year a new model would be introduced, but the car was essentially unchanged. A new chrome ornament plus redesigned taillight plus pinstriping does not equal improvement. These are changes, maybe appealing changes, but nevertheless merely changes. Likewise, education goes from change to change to change without any data on improvement. Often these changes are written into law. For example, some states require new textbooks to be adopted every six or seven years. It is assumed that the change from the old textbook to the new textbook will be an improvement; but in fact it is only a change, without one shred of evidence that the new textbook resulted in any improvement. Change is a neutral word; it can represent a positive or a negative. Improvement, on the other hand, is defined as positive change.

How does one know if improvement has occurred? Two indicators must be in place before a change can be declared an improvement: There must be fewer failures and more successes. Ideally, there is also less variation. Figure 2-1 displays two bell-shaped curves. The solid line represents the status of an organization before a change. The dotted line represents improvement.

The two curves could represent high school seniors, for example. In this case, the left of both curves represent students who are in prison or who have dropped out of school; the right of both curves represent students entering a university with advanced placement credit. An academic change at the high school can be declared an improvement when there are (1) fewer dropouts, and (2) more students with advanced placement credit. Less variability in student accomplishment is also desirable.

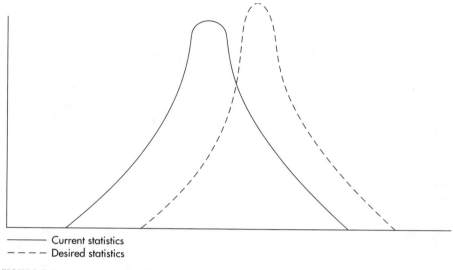

Current statistics
— — — Desired statistics

FIGURE 2-1. Improvement on the normal, bell-shaped curve.

Often organizations declare that an improvement has occurred when only the lower or the upper end of the curve has changed. For example, if a school has fewer dropouts, common sense would indicate this is improvement. One cannot tell, however, by looking at only the lower end of the curve. The school might have redirected resources to decrease dropouts but had far fewer students well prepared for the university. Such is merely a change in emphasis; it is not an improvement of the high school.

At other times organizations declare that an improvement has occurred if the average exam score rises. This is a deceiving statistic. It is possible for a high school to raise the average score on an exam and at the same time have more dropouts. If five more students drop out of school and 10 more score slightly higher on an exam, the average might go up, but the high school has not improved.

Bright ideas appear constantly, but they should not be implemented right away. The bright idea decision must be delayed. First the organization members must gather data on the current situation. For example, somebody has a concept for improving discipline at recess. First the staff must gather data on what discipline the current system is producing. How many students are referred to the office in a year? How many students have had zero referrals, one referral, two referrals, three referrals, and more than three referrals? The current system is represented by the solid line on the bell-shaped curve in Figure 2-1. The left end represents those students who are referred to the office more than three times. The right end represents those students who are never referred to the office for discipline. The appropriate time to listen to a bright idea is when the current system is documented.

If the changes from the bright idea result in improvement, then fewer students will be sent to the office more than three times a year, more students will have no referrals, and ideally the range will be narrower. Figures 2-2 and 2-3 show a hypothetical school of 500 students. Figure 2-2 represents the educational output before the change. Figure 2-3 represents the output after the change. In this hypothetical situation it can be declared that improvement has occurred because fewer students are at the lower end, more are at the upper end, and there is less variation among the student body.

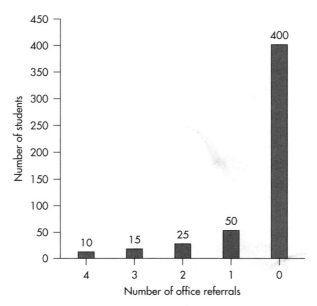

FIGURE 2-2.   Discipline before change in hypothetical school.

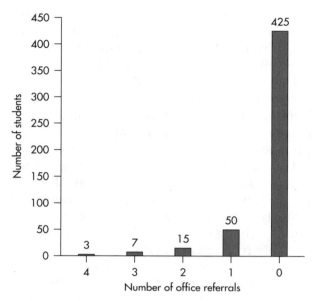

FIGURE 2-3. Discipline after change in hypothetical school.

Figures 2-4 through 2-8 provide an actual history of first grade reading improvement. In the spring of 1992 all Enterprise School District (Redding, California) first graders read a 100-word story. Their errors were counted and recorded. This assessment occurred before a change in district instructional strategy was made. The following year, in the second semester, first graders struggling with reading were provided, through federal Title I funds, a personal tutor for 20 to 30 minutes a day. The same structure was used for the 1993–94 school year. In 1994–95 another change was made: The one-on-one tutoring service began in September. Each year more students were successful (less than 21 errors) and fewer experienced failure (71 or more errors). Thus, the changes in reading instruction resulted in improvement. Future changes are to be judged by the same criteria to see if they result in even more improvement.

As of this writing, district staff are stating that the standards for failure and success must be raised, as they no longer match teacher expectations. Only students making fewer than 10 errors are considered successful and students making 31 or more errors are considered to be experiencing failure and in need of Title I services.

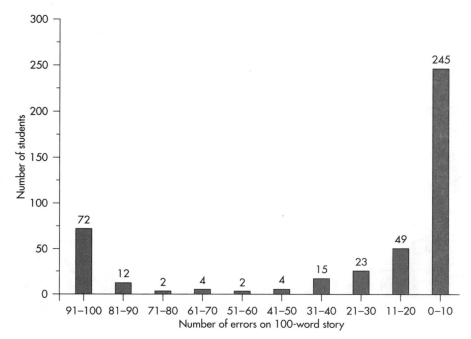

FIGURE 2-4. First grade reading in 1992.

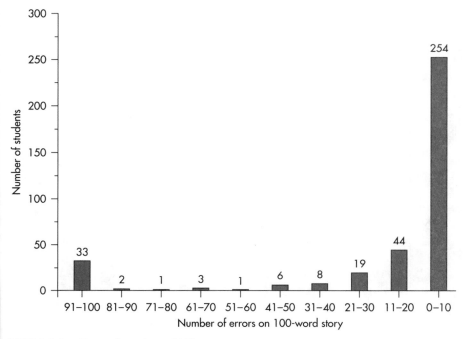

FIGURE 2-5. First grade reading in 1993.

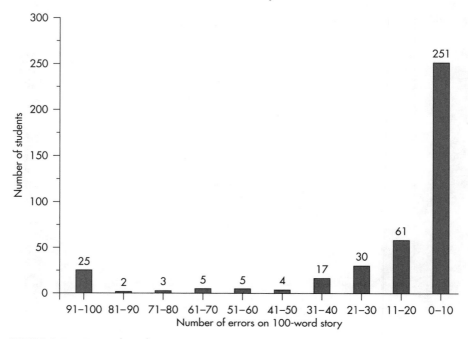

FIGURE 2-6. First grade reading in 1994.

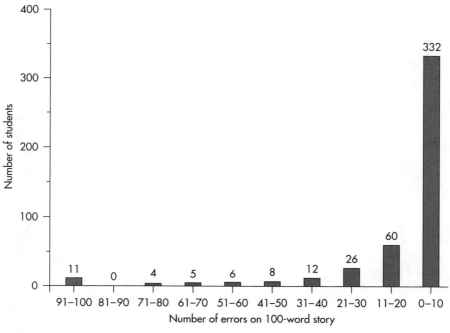

FIGURE 2-7. First grade reading in 1995.

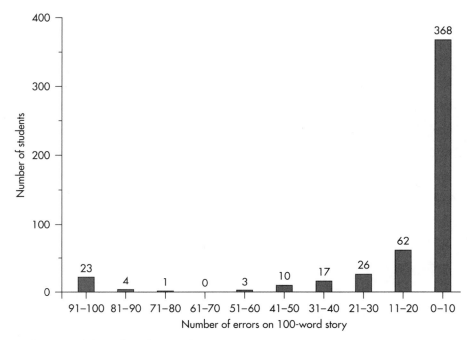

FIGURE 2-8. First grade reading in 1996.

Figure 2-9 illustrates a hypothetical history of standards, variation, and improvement. At stage 1 the majority of students demonstrate learning at a level below the standard. Through improvement efforts, the majority of students achieve the standard (stages 2, 3, and 4) until, at stage 5, all students are above the standard. Stage 6 shows the establishment of a new standard with an old one in place for comparison purposes.

Figure 2-8 was obviously not good news. After three years of continuous improvement, a year of regression is welcomed by nobody. As a superintendent I was disappointed. As an author, however, I am not disappointed. A year of discouraging results is reality in the difficult journey to improve student learning. Several lessons were learned from analysis of the 1996 data, but the most significant lesson is that all beginning readers must be monitored regularly so no one falls through the cracks.

Figure 2-10 is a record of reading progress for five years. Even though Figure 2-8 showed no improvement in first grade reading,

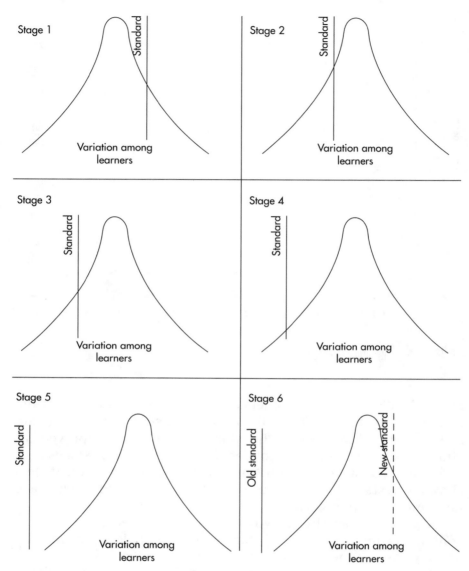

FIGURE 2-9.   History of standards, variation, and improvement.

teachers still wanted to raise standards. The last pair of columns show students' failure and success according to revised, more difficult standards.

Dr. Deming fully recognized that teachers and other leaders have much to manage. They cannot set aside all their time to work on improvement. He wrote, "We must of course solve problems and

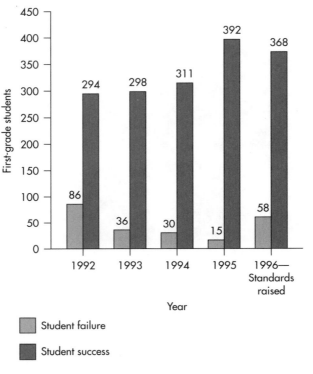

FIGURE 2-10. First-grade reading, 1992–1996.

stamp out fires as they occur, but these activities do not change the system."[1] It is a deep sense of purpose that propels leaders to manage resources and time so that all energy is not used up stamping out fires.

The three building blocks for improving schools are (1) a commitment to stop blaming; (2) the establishment of clear aims; and (3) agreement on a definition of improvement. Dr. Deming's profound knowledge, discussed in the next section, makes the truth of these basics even more apparent.

Note

1. W. Edwards Deming, *Schools and Communities Cooperating for Quality—Lessons for Leaders* (seminar sponsored by American Association of School Administrators, Alexandria, Va., 1990, handout), ch. 4, p. 2.

Section II
Deming's Profound Knowledge

Knowledge that the prevailing style of management must change is necessary but not sufficient. We must know what changes to make. Profound knowledge appears in four parts: appreciation for a system, theory of variation, theory of knowledge, and psychology.[1] In Dr. Deming's last book, The New Economics, *he outlined his management philosophy as divided into these four categories. The four following chapters are not intended to compete with the complete thoughts of Dr. Deming, but are meant as a commentary and bridge between Dr. Deming's thoughts and educational applications.*

Chapter 3
SYSTEM

Merit pay for teachers makes sense. Why not pay exemplary teachers more money? After all, in other professions those who work a 10-to-12-hour day generally earn more money than those who work a 6-to-8-hour day. Some teachers are inferior and almost everyone knows who they are. Some teachers are average; they meet the needs of half of the students. But some teachers are exemplary; they meet the needs of all students with maybe an occasional failure. So why not pay them more?

The faulty logic behind merit pay proposals is the same inadequate thinking supporting most educational reform. The nonsystem thinking purports to improve the whole of education by tinkering with some parts of the system. Merit pay advocates naively believe that changing the salary schedule will improve learning. (Unions often have the same belief, just a different concept of change to the salary schedule.)

Recently I spent a weekend with a membership organization's board of directors. For the last five years the organization has been losing members. Because of this failure the board was most willing to listen to Dr. Deming's philosophy. A synopsis of my questions and the board's answers follows:

Q: What has your sales record been like the past five years?

A: Between 8 percent and 10 percent new customers each year.

Q: How about lost members?

A: We've been losing approximately 12 percent of our membership each year.

Q: What are your current plans to improve?

A: We are providing a free trip to Hawaii for each salesperson who meets his or her quota [merit pay]. If all sales staff meet their quota, we'll reverse the downward spiral.

Q: Is the trip incentive working?

A: It is too soon to tell, but 40 percent to 60 percent of the sales staff seem discouraged, believing they'll never meet their quota.

Q: What is your biggest problem? Obtaining new members or keeping current members?

A: Keeping members.

Q: Which members of your staff have the most to do with keeping members?

A: Office staff

Q: Not the sales staff?

A: No.

Q: Is the office staff afforded the opportunity to win a trip to Hawaii?

A: No.

Q: Why?

A: We haven't looked at the whole company this way. We thought the solution to our problem was more sales.

Q: If the problem is net loss of members, wouldn't it be better if everybody could go to Hawaii when the five-year trend of losing members is reversed?

A: That means the secretaries might go to Hawaii? We hadn't considered this.

Q: Does this line of questioning help you understand a little of Dr. Deming's thinking about a system?

A: Yes

I'm writing now at 30,000 feet. One requirement for completion of this book is a safe landing. The whole air transportation system must work together for a safe landing. I have little interest in a bonus for the pilot if the mechanics didn't do their job correctly. Everyone understands the need for the whole air transportation system to work together because the flights begin and end within a period of a few hours.

The school system, however, starts and ends over a 13-year period. Public schooling will survive the current crisis only when the whole system improves. Customers (students) and stakeholders (parents) must have a system that works together to produce quality high school graduates. Most reform efforts address only a subsystem. Merit pay, for example, makes only a few people happy. Charter schools allow some children to attend a different school (not necessarily better) for a few years. A charter school spanning all grades, K–12, has the opportunity to address system improvement, but other charter schools are only tinkering with a subsystem of education. Dropout prevention programs are also a subsystem. Special and bilingual education are subsystems. Anyone can cite attempts to improve subsystems, often at the expense of the whole system.

When Dr. Deming suggested replacing the traditional organizational chart with a system view, he diagrammed a profound school restructuring vision. His system view of organizations published in 1986 is the foundation for the education system view shown in Figure 3-1.

Dr. Deming's system view had only one input location. My variation of his system view for education has two input locales—one for the supply and one for the K–12 system itself. Education improvement depends not only on improved input to the system, but improved input to the supply.

A system is a network of components within an organization that work together for the aim of the organization.[2] Note that all seven system elements are included on the system diagram in Figure 3-1. The paragraphs that follow explain the seven elements and contrast the system diagram with the traditional organizational chart.

1. *Education has customers.* The word *customer* is not on traditional organizational charts. Education's customers are the students. As K–12 organizations study quality in more detail, their members identify more customers, such as universities, employers, teachers at the next grade level, and other external and internal customers. These discussions are healthy once consensus has been reached that the students are the prime customers: They live the rest of their lives with the services they receive in the K–12 school system.

2. *Education needs an aim.* Aim is not on traditional organizational charts. Education currently has many people working toward their own aims.

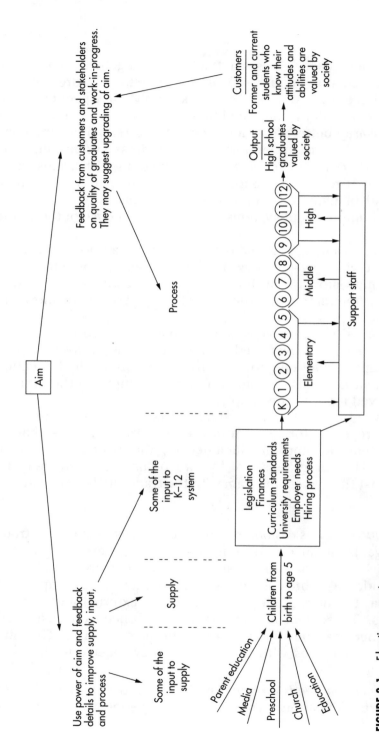

FIGURE 3-1. Education as a system.

3. *Education can improve its supply.* Suppliers are not on traditional organizational charts. Educators often think there's nothing they can do about supply. They must accept all children who live within their school district boundaries. The second sentence is true, but the first is not. Whatever the aim of education, it is in the best interest of school districts to assign some of their most talented teachers to helping parents and preschool teachers better prepare students for school success.

4. *Process: Grade levels must be linked.* Only the job classification of the teacher is on the traditional organizational chart, not the process and grade levels. The amount of time necessary to coordinate education between grade levels is no more than the amount of time necessary to coordinate the design of the components of an automobile.

5. *Education has output.* Output is not mentioned on traditional organizational charts. Education produces graduates qualified for universities, colleges, and technical schools and also produces graduates prepared neither technologically nor for college admission. Education also produces dropouts. The term *produce* is repulsive to educators because Americans live in a blaming society. Some students have never been read to by an adult outside school; some have little or no love; some are abused; some move every three months; and many are full of alcohol, tobacco, and other toxins. Educators don't want to be blamed for society's failures. Educators do, however, have the responsibility to improve education, which quite simply means producing fewer unprepared graduates, fewer dropouts, and more prepared graduates. Nobody believes that all dropouts will be eliminated or that every student will graduate prepared for university education, but gradual, continual improvement in graduate production is attainable.

6. *Education needs quality measurement.* Quality measurement is not mentioned on traditional organizational charts. State laws mandate that teachers be evaluated by their principals. This has limited value. Instead, legislators should demand that school boards orchestrate the collection of quality measurements from their customers and stakeholders.

7. *Education has input. Most is from state and federal government.* Input is not mentioned on traditional organizational charts. Legislators need to view education as a system for which

they are responsible. Educators are not in control of the education system; it is controlled by noneducators elected to the legislatures or placed in judicial chairs. Dr. Deming frequently asked, "Who has the most control over a ship crossing the ocean?" After captain, engine room boss, and navigator were rejected as answers, he said, "The designer of the ship. The ship can never do better than its design will allow."[3]

Legislators designed the education ship. They legislate what the government will pay for (attendance, collective bargaining, grant awards, and so on); the requirements to be a teacher or administrator; the requirements to fire a teacher or administrator; the number of school days the government will pay for each year; that the demands of special education attorneys must be met no matter what the effect on other students; and thousands of other rules that require compliance. Legislatures control much of the input.

The elements of a system are aim, supply, input, process, output, customer, and quality measurement. If any one of the elements is missing, there is no system—only parts. Since improvement is the goal, all seven elements must be studied. All components of the system must work together toward the aim of the system. Dr. Deming called all components working together *optimization. Suboptimization,* as in merit pay or special interest legislation, is one part of the system winning at the expense of the whole.

Notes

1. W. Edwards Deming, *Schools and Communities Cooperating for Quality—Lessons for Leaders* (seminar sponsored by American Association of School Administrators, Alexandria, Va., 1990, handout), ch. 4, p. 1.
2. Ibid, ch. 4, p. 5.
3. W. Edwards Deming, American Association of School Administrators Conference, Washington, D.C., January, 1992.

Chapter 4
EPISTEMOLOGY (THEORY OF KNOWLEDGE)

Dr. Deming has a very useful classification of content to be learned. Often educators use the term *what students know and can do.* Dr. Deming's use of the simple words *information* and *knowledge* is much more meaningful in designing educational improvement.

Dr. Deming defined information as facts about the past.[1] A dictionary is full of information, yet it has no knowledge. Spelling is a subject studied in schools that relates the past to today's youth. It communicates how people in the past agreed to spell particular words. Knowledge, by contrast, is about the future. Writing is a subject studied in schools that is about the future: How can something be written so readers in the future will better understand? Students who become proficient in writing can help create a better future for themselves and others.

Every subject taught in schools has both information and knowledge. The educational pendulum swings to and fro, placing emphasis on information and then knowledge and then back to information. The reality is that both knowledge and information have importance and need clear aims.

The following provides some examples of information and knowledge gained from school subjects.

Subject	Information	Knowledge
Mathematics	Concepts	Problem solving
Language	Spelling; pronunciation	Writing; reading with understanding
Art	Technique identification	Producing own work
Business Education	Check writing	Balancing an account
Science	Definitions	Using scientific method

Subject	Information	Knowledge
History	Chronology	Relating current events to past
Geography	Locations	Relating economy to geography
Music	Composer identification	Producing music

The quality measurements described in *Improving Student Learning* are equally valid for measuring both information and knowledge.

The key elements of Dr. Deming's epistemological thinking are

1. Information is about the past; knowledge is necessary to create a better future.
2. Learn from the masters; they are few.
3. Only one example contrary to a theory is necessary to cause revision of the theory.
4. Learning comes from testing theories. "Without theory there is no learning, and thus no improvement—only motion."[2]
5. Knowledge is necessary to better predict the future.
6. The responsibility of leaders is to create more leaders.
7. Experience alone gives no knowledge.

In time, elements 2 through 7 may eclipse element 1 in educational importance. Today, however, the educational need of the United States is to stop the swinging pendulum. The terms used for the two pendulum directions are *conservative* and *liberal.* These two emotionally laden words must be replaced with the neutral words *information* and *knowledge.* Student success in both information and knowledge is the responsibility of all educators.

Even though education is in the knowledge business, most educational practices run contrary to the seven key epistemological elements. For example, many educators never have the opportunity to learn for even a week from a master. Instead, their in-service experiences are composed of listening to a speaker for an hour or attending a workshop on how to use a newly published textbook.

Another example of an educational practice that runs contrary to Dr. Deming's epistemological postulates relates to writing instruction. A common theory held by many teachers is that they should not help a student with spelling while he or she is writing a first draft. They tell the student to do his or her best; editing comes later. The theory is that attention paid to spelling in the first draft will cause the young writer to lose creativity and productivity. According to Dr. Deming only one example contrary to this theory would be necessary to demand its revision. Only one child is needed whose writing creativity is damaged and productivity lessened by a teacher's refusal to help with spelling during the writing of a first draft. Likely every teacher knows of a perfectionist child who needs to know spelling *right now* or both creativity and production are lessened. Therefore the theory of spelling assistance must be revised. Perhaps an additional theory should be, "Some children will write more creatively and produce more text when they can attend to spelling during the first draft."

If Dr. Deming were writing this chapter, he probably would have spent time focusing on element 4. It is theory, not experience, that enables one to learn. The purpose of experience is to validate or challenge a theory. Throughout *Improving Student Learning*, graphs of student work are shown. Dr. Deming would have teachers use all their knowledge and the wisdom of master teachers to develop a theory about how to improve student learning. The results shown in the graphs either validate that the theory worked and improved learning occurred, or they challenge the theory. Without theory and data the teacher and students move through yet another school year with no improvement in the classroom system.

Oh, that we could change the term *educator* to *epistemologist.*

Notes

1. W. Edwards Deming, *The New Economics* (Cambridge, Mass.: MIT Press, 1993).
2. W. Edwards Deming, *Schools and Communities Cooperating for Quality—Lessons for Leaders* (seminar sponsored by American Association of School Administrators, Alexandria, Va., 1990, handout), ch. 3, p. 2.

Chapter 5
PSYCHOLOGY

Never did I expect to pick up books written by a person who spent most of his career advising manufacturers and clarify my thinking on child psychology. Prior to reading Dr. Deming I had questions, but no coherent theory. I questioned the motivation admonition given to teachers. I seriously wondered if it was the responsibility of teachers to artificially motivate students. When my preparation matched student interests, students were motivated; and when my preparation had nothing to do with what the students wanted to learn, my motivation tricks failed. Dr. Deming provided a coherent, simple psychology theory.

Instead of thinking that one must motivate children, Dr. Deming reminded that all children are born motivated. Educators are meant not to motivate children to learn, but to discover what demotivates them, and stop those practices. He wrote, "We have been destroying our people, from toddlers on through the university, and on the job. We must preserve the power of intrinsic motivation, dignity, cooperation, curiosity, joy in learning, that people are born with. . . . All the qualities that have been traditionally and erroneously applied to competition actually apply better to cooperation. Cooperation builds character, is basic to human nature, and makes learning more enjoyable and productive."[1] America's obsession with competition is destroying the inborn motivation to learn.

The basic tenets of Western-society management destroy natural motivation. All of the tricks that are designed to motivate children actually have the opposite effect—they demotivate. Examples of such tricks are prizes for reading, stickers for completed work, grades, money for grades, and graphs comparing children's progress.

David Elkind wrote, "One of the most serious and pernicious misunderstandings about young children is that they are most like adults in their thinking and least like us in their feelings. In fact, just the reverse is true, and children are most like us in their feelings and least like us in their thinking."[2]

It really isn't difficult to determine what has the long-term effect of destroying student motivation. Try out the practice on the teachers first. If it demotivates teachers, then it will demotivate students. Even if children are initially excited about a prize, the long-term effect on children will be the same as the long-term effect on teachers. For example, if a school has a problem with teachers forgetting their duties, the principal could put up a chart in the staff room with the name of each teacher. Stickers would be placed daily next to the names of the teachers who remember their duties. If the staff room chart motivates teachers to dedicate themselves even more deeply to their profession, then the same technique will help children keep their inborn motivation for learning.

Once teachers internalize that (1) everyone is born motivated; (2) the management techniques they have observed throughout their lives demotivate; and (3) whatever demotivates adults also demotivates children, they are ready to use with students only the management techniques they want their principals to use on them.

Students are on a 13-year formal learning train. Those who reach the graduation depot having completed advanced placement courses are extremely well prepared for the world-class economy. The name of the track that takes the learning train to the depot is *motivation.* Students enter kindergarten with a complete track ahead of them. Adults and the culture of schooling systematically dismantle the railroad ties until few students have a working track by age 18. It's very simple—no track equals a derailed learning train.

Beyond the facts that all children are born motivated to learn and educators have the responsibility to maintain this enthusiasm, Dr. Deming provides five other key psychological truths.

1. Most people, once discouraged, stay that way. How often do people say, "I loved math in grades 2, 5, and 8?" What everybody normally hears is, "I loved math until grade $x,$ and then I never liked it again."

2. Children don't destroy their own motivation; adults do. These adults can be teachers, cooks, secretaries, church leaders, scout volunteers, parents, or other relatives.

3. There's no shortage of good people unless people create it. No teachers set out to create a shortage of good adults. It is safe to say, however, that almost every teacher is part of a K–12 system using Western-society management techniques that systematically create shortages of good people.

4. Ranking destroys joy. No adult I'm aware of wants to be publicly ranked *bad* in anything. Even in a simple game of Scrabble, no one wants to be ranked last. Sure, the pain of losing at Scrabble is over in two minutes, but adults still don't like it. Consider being ranked for something important. The major way educators rank is with grades. Grades destroy joy. Destruction of joy destroys learning. Built into Dr. Deming's complete theories are the necessary tools to eliminate ranking through grades while, at the same time, being more accountable to the public.

5. The customer defines joy. When I am the customer at a restaurant, I determine whether the dining experience was joyful. I am the customer. In schools, the students define joy. It is the students' morale that must be of prime importance.

The memory of Education 101 must disappear. Future teachers need no longer be admonished to motivate as a part of every lesson plan. Dr. Deming's simple psychology must replace Education 101. Life comes with built-in motivation.

Notes

1. W. Edwards Deming, *Schools and Communities Cooperating for Quality—Lessons for Leaders* (seminar sponsored by American Association of School Administrators, Alexandria, Va., 1990, handout), ch. 4, pp. 1, 14.
2. David Elkind, *Children and Adolescents* (New York: Oxford University Press, 1974), p. 51.

Chapter 6
VARIATION

Every teacher knows the frustration caused by the wide range of ability in a single classroom. Kindergarten teachers face five-year-olds who know how to read and other five-year-olds who don't know if a book is upside down or not. High schools have both students reading like an average third grader (usually these become dropouts) and students earning college credit while still in high school.

Some students attend the same school system for the 13 years of their K–12 education. Some students attend 50 or more schools in 13 years. Some students are rarely absent; others are rarely present. Members of service clubs know this. After spending their entire lunch complaining about the morning's poorly written job applications, they award a $1000 college scholarship to an incredibly talented 17-year-old senior.

Variation is the enemy of education; it is also the enemy of business. The quality of service and product varies among different stores in the same chain. Not all products manufactured from the same factory, on the same day, operate equally well.

Variation is such a problem that Dr. Deming wrote, "The central problem of management . . . is to understand the meaning of variation, and to extract the information contained in variation."[1]

Understanding variation means educators must accept that variation will always be present. No amount of educational research, reform, or referendum will eliminate variation. Some variation is caused by unusual events; some variation is built into the system; and some is just luck, both good and bad. Variation *is*.

Even though variation *is,* leaders have the responsibility to reduce it. When teachers first hear this they are repulsed because they think uniqueness is to be reduced. Nothing could be further from the truth. Uniqueness is prized. Uniqueness is not a problem; variation is the problem that must be reduced.

For example, a fifth grade teacher might have students whose reading abilities range from that of an average first grader to that of

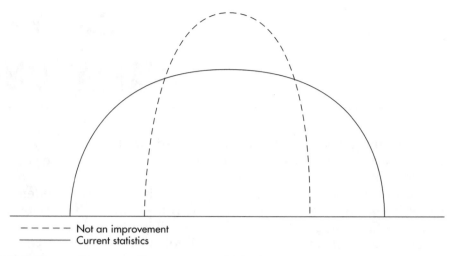

- - - - - Not an improvement
————— Current statistics

FIGURE 6-1. The opposite of Dr. Deming's view of reduced variation.

an average 11th grader. Reducing variation in reading would improve education.

Not so, say the parents of students who are reading at high levels. The picture they have of reducing variation is Figure 6-1, which is the opposite of Dr. Deming's view of improvement and reducing variation (see Figure 2-1 in Chapter 2).

Yes, the poorest students are to be helped, but not at the expense of the better readers. Figure 6-1 is *not* what Dr. Deming meant by reducing variation. Decisions that take away from one part of the organization and give to another part of the organization are not improvement; they are merely a shift of resources. Figure 6-1 represents an economic picture of socialism, which in no way represents Dr. Deming's thinking.

In Figure 2-1, fifth graders' reading ability (first grade through 11th grade level) is represented by the solid line. The dotted line represents Dr. Deming's idea of reduced variation, which shows that after an improvement, fifth grade classes had students reading between the third and 12th grade levels. The variation is reduced from 10 grades (11 – 1) to 9 grades (12 – 3). Dr. Deming's concept of reducing variation encompasses improvement whereby there is not only a reduction of variation, but fewer failures and more successes.

The seven key elements of Dr. Deming's statistical thinking are as follows:

1. Variation is always present.
2. Variation is the enemy.
3. The purpose of statistics is to help decision makers reduce variation.
4. The key responsibility of management is to reduce variation.
5. Through the use of statistical control charts managers can determine whether variation is caused by special events outside the system or by common causes within the system.
6. Ninety-seven percent of what occurs in organizations *cannot* be measured but must be managed anyway.
7. Through statistics one can more nearly predict the future. For example, if one knows the number of dropouts in a school district for the past 10 years, one can predict the number of dropouts next year with greater precision.

"Management is about the future; nobody should be paid much for counting up the past."[2] The required statistics in most undergraduate and graduate courses help educators count up the past. Quality measurement is completely different; it's about creating a better future.

According to Dr. Deming, there are three sources of power: (1) formal; (2) knowledge; and (3) personality and persuasive power.

A successful manager of people develops 2 and 3; does not rely on 1. He has nevertheless an obligation to use 1, as this source of power enables him to change the system—equipment, materials, methods—to bring improvement. He is in authority, but if lacking knowledge or personality he must depend upon his power. He unconsciously fills a void in his qualifications by making it clear to everybody that his is a position of authority.[3]

Teachers, principals, superintendents, board members, and other leaders are all tempted to use power too often. It is well understood in education that personality and persuasion are valuable tools, but knowledge is the other key resource to keep from abusing power. Dr. Deming's profound knowledge fills a vacuum in educational knowledge. Table 6-1 provides a summary of profound knowledge.

TABLE 6-1.   Summary of profound knowledge.

System	Epistemology	Psychology	Variation
Aim	Information about the past	People are born motivated.	Always present
Customers	Knowledge for a better future	Once discouraged, most stay that way.	The enemy
Supply	Learn from masters	Adults destroy motivation.	Statistics reduce variation.
Input	One contrary example equals wrong theory.	Society creates a shortage of good people.	Primary responsibility of management
Process	Better predict the future with knowledge	Ranking destroys joy.	Special- and common-cause variation
Output	Create more leaders.	Customer defines joy.	97% of occurrences cannot be measured.
Quality measurement	Experience alone provides no knowledge.		Statistics help managers better predict the future.

Notes

1. W. Edwards Deming, *Out of the Crisis* (Cambridge, Mass.: MIT Press, 1986), p. 20.
2. W. Edwards Deming, American Association of School Administrators, Washington, D.C., January, 1992.
3. W. Edwards Deming, *Schools and Communities Cooperating for Quality—Lessons for Leaders* (seminar sponsored by American Association of School Administrators, Alexandria, Va., 1990, handout), ch. 6, p. 6.

Section III
Improving Learning

Dr. Deming never understood why education adopted the statistics of athletics. These statistical methods are perfect for games in which the objective is to have one winner and many losers. One college wins the annual basketball Final Four; all other U.S. colleges are losers. No long-term harm is caused by creating so many losers because basketball is only a game.

Education is not a game. Millions of winners are needed in education. Educators know the aim of education is to have as many winners as possible, but prior to Dr. Deming's teachings educators knew no other statistics existed for education. The following six chapters are devoted to examples and explanations of quality measurement appropriate for education and millions of young winners.

Chapter 7
MEASURING INFORMATION

Every subject has important information educated persons should know. Even when students have wristwatches connected to the Internet, knowing the basic information encompassed in every subject is expected of educated people. The most important aspect of measuring information is clearly articulating to students and their parents the information to be learned by a designated time. For example, a second grade teacher can state to her students that they are expected to know how to spell the 1000 most-often used English words by the end of eighth grade. In second grade they are expected to know how to spell the first 200 words.

In current educational practice, teachers seldom clearly state what information is to be known at the end of a course. Most often the course begins with students having only a foggy notion of what they are to learn. Sometimes the assignments are clearly stated, but what is to be learned is not settled in the students' minds. The educational practice closest to having a clear aim is the pretest, weekly test, posttest sequence of events because the pretest gives students some idea of what lies ahead.

Four problems, however, exist with the pretest, weekly test, posttest scenario.

1. The posttest gives the teacher information at the year's end, when it is too late to adjust instructional strategies. What has been learned has been learned and what has not been learned will not be learned that particular year.

2. The teacher doesn't really know from weekly reviews or tests what the students have learned. The cram factor greatly influences the results. Students who are good at cramming for tests can trick the teacher into thinking they know something they don't know.

3. The teacher has no ongoing information on the progress of the class. There is merely a grand hope that the posttest will show improvement over the pretest.

4. The biggest problem with the traditional scenario is that the teacher has limited responsibility for the students' learning. The teacher teaches, the students may or may not learn, and the teacher evaluates.

In a 1992 seminar sponsored by the American Association of School Administrators, Dr. Deming suggested a radically different way to manage learning. The steps he suggested follow. Second grade spelling, with 200 words for the year, is used as an example to elaborate on the steps.

- Explain to the students the aim of the course. This advice matches the first of his 14 points for management, which is to maintain constancy of purpose.[1]
- Quiz the students on the square root of the total number of words each week (14 is the approximate square root of 200).
- Each week, randomly select items for the quiz. The students are not told the items prior to the quiz because they will cram, and the teacher will not really know if the students are learning. Spreadsheet programs can generate a list of random numbers, but students often prefer to see how the words are selected. An enjoyable way to do this is to write each of the 200 spelling words on a small card, place all of the cards in a bag, and let 14 students each week draw a card. This way students know the teacher didn't trick them if a disproportionate number of difficult words appear on a particular quiz.
- Two basic classroom graphs to be generated by the teacher are a class run chart and class scatter diagram. A third graph, the student run chart, is described in Chapter 10. Build a run chart (line graph) for classroom display. The run chart displays the total number of items correct for the whole class. A perfect score for a classroom of 30 pupils tested on 14 spelling words a week is 420 (see Figure 7-1). The posted line graph communicates to students progress toward the goal. Children can identify reasons for sudden decreases, such as many absences, difficult words, being excited about an upcoming field trip, or other distractions. They can also experience the joy of classroom success and their individual contribution toward the goal.
- Build a scatter diagram such as that shown in Figure 7-2. The graph personalizes the data in that each dot represents a student.

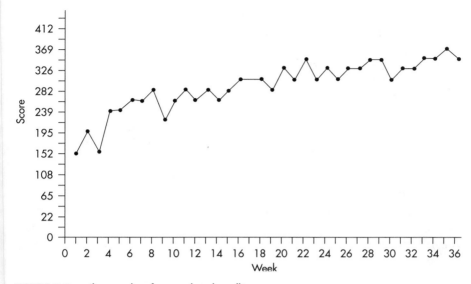

FIGURE 7-1.   Class run chart for second grade spelling.

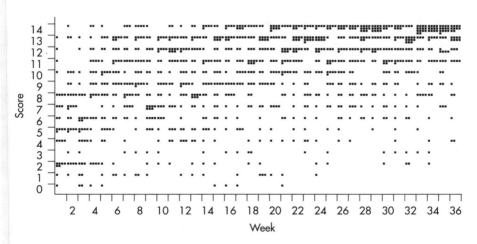

FIGURE 7-2.   Class scatter diagram for second grade spelling.

More than any other quality tool it speaks to the heart of a teacher who desires that none of the students fail. The traditional statistical approach of reporting averages masks both failures and exceptional successes. The scatter diagram is for teacher study, whereas the class run chart is for both students and the teacher.

Figures 7-3 and 7-4 are the first complete run chart and scatter diagram ever completed according to Dr. Deming's recommendation. Damon Cropsey, a fifth grade teacher in California's Enterprise School District selected 100 locations in the United States that he wanted his students to know. In addition to the 50 states, his students learned the location of 50 rivers, cities, mountains, and lakes. Note that the least knowledgeable students moved from one correct to seven correct at year's end; the largest group of students was 100 percent successful; and variation was reduced from a range of seven to three.

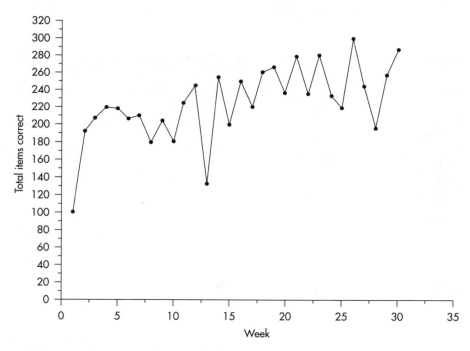

FIGURE 7-3. Class run chart for fifth grade geography.

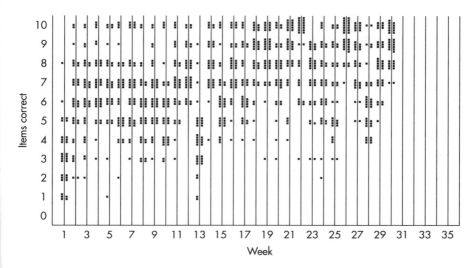

FIGURE 7-4. Class scatter diagram for fifth grade geography.

Figure 7-5 documents reading improvement in a first grade classroom of 30 students. The data show the students' success at reading 100 high-frequency words. Each week, 10 of the 100 words were randomly selected and the children were asked one at a time to read the words. The run chart shows the total number of words read by the whole class each week.

The scatter diagram shown in Figure 7-6 displays a dot for each week for each student. Note that in week 1 most of the students were able to read none of the words; by week 36 the same number of students could read all 10 words.

Often when teachers see the power of this approach to learning they desire to connect the learning of several years in a very structured way. After seeing Damon Cropsey's fifth grade graphs, fourth grade teachers selected 100 map locations they wanted their students to know. They used a 100-sided die[2] to randomly select 10 locations each week. The fourth graders were provided blank maps of their county, state, the United States, North America, and the world. One hundred locations relating to California history were numbered. (The maps are shown in Figures 7-7

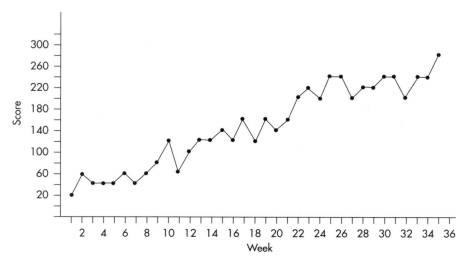

FIGURE 7-5. Class run chart for first grade reading.

through 7-11). After each roll of the die, students wrote the name of the location on a paper labeled 1 to 10.

The fifth grade geography list was edited to eliminate duplicate locations and 100 new locations were selected for sixth grade. The directions circulated to teachers are provided in Appendix A. Data were collected from all fifth grade classrooms; the results are given in Chapter 9 and 11.

Teachers working together toward a common aim is powerful. In the words of Kevin Jenkins (no relation), "Today's successful leader realizes that innovation creates opportunity, quality creates demand, and teamwork makes it happen."[3]

Even though they do not include data for a complete year, Figures 7-12 and 7-13 document the same tools at work in physical fitness. The run chart (Figure 7-12) shows the total number of laps run by a class, while the scatter diagram (Figure 7-13) shows a dot for each runner each week. Figures 7-14 and 7-15 are also for a portion of a year, but show a new subject to this story: science. This example demonstrates that the right time to begin the quality improvement process is *now*. The science data are from only the last 12 weeks of a school year because the teacher learned of this process 12 weeks before school ended. Even though this teacher used a hectic time of the year to learn a new process, he is far ahead for next year.

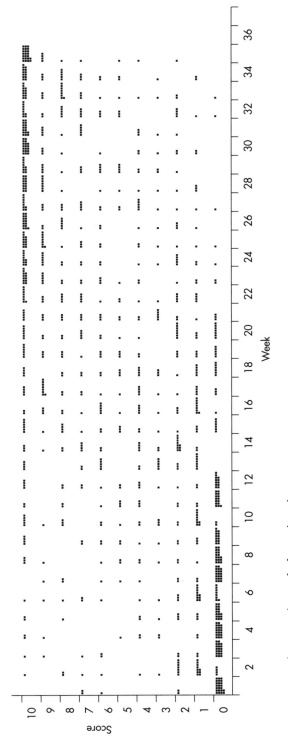

FIGURE 7-6. Class scatter diagram for first grade reading.

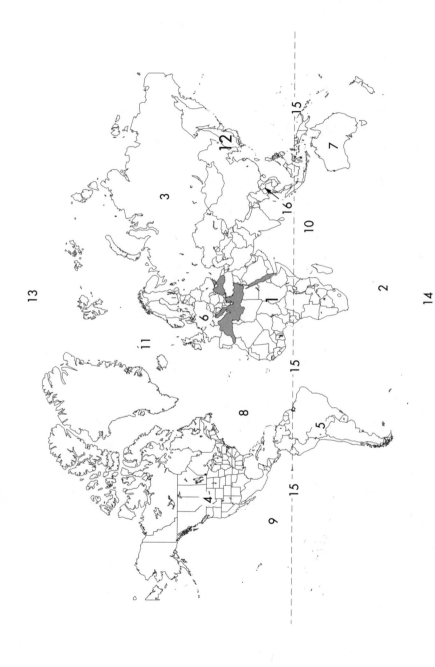

FIGURE 7-7. World map with numbered locations.

FIGURE 7-8. North America map with numbered locations.

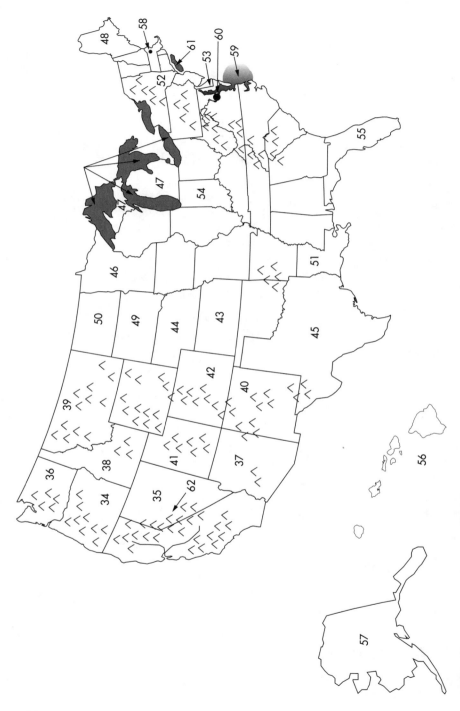

FIGURE 7-9. U.S. map with numbered locations.

46

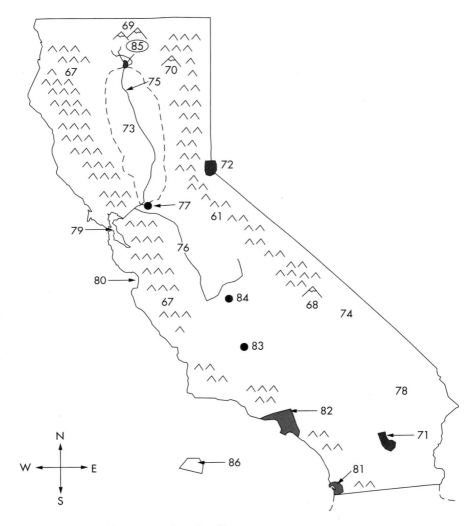

FIGURE 7-10. California map with numbered locations.

Dr. Deming was clear on the difference between evaluation and feedback. Evaluation is what the boss says, feedback is what the customers say. Improvement occurs, in Dr. Deming's opinion, when managers pay very close attention to feedback. If his way were followed, all of America's managers would replace evaluation with feedback from the customer.[4] Dr. Deming set the standard very high when he wrote, "[A leader] will hold a conversation of four hours

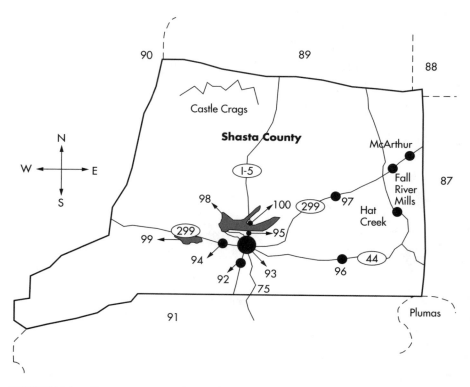

FIGURE 7-11.   Shasta County map with numbered locations.

with every one of his people, at least once a year, not for judgment, but to listen."[5] Most educators would like their bosses to follow this advice. Students would also like their teachers to listen. The statistical feedback described in this chapter does not replace actual conversations, but it is conscientious, concerted, regular listening to students. Feedback is advocated—feedback from the student-customers.

With evaluation as the goal, the teacher gives assignments to the students, gives them time to study, tests them, and then evaluates them on their success. When the goal is improvement, the teacher believes that the person with the major responsibility for student success is the teacher. The students are held responsible for doing the work, but the students cannot change the system operating within the classroom. Only the teacher has the power to change the classroom system. Therefore, if the system is not working and the students are not making satisfactory progress

Seventh grade physical education, six-minute run

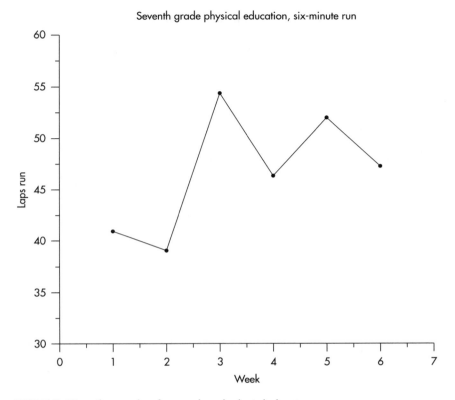

FIGURE 7-12. Class run chart for seventh grade physical education.

toward the instructional aims, then the teacher must improve the instructional system. By sharing feedback, the teacher and students plan together different instructional strategies so that the students can learn successfully. A topic for a class meeting might be, "Why has our geography run chart declined for the last three weeks? Do we need to do anything differently? If so, what?"

If teachers have evaluation in their minds, quizzing students every week on the content to be known at the end of the course is cruel. How can the students be evaluated on content they have not yet been taught? They can't, at least not fairly. Dr. Deming was not suggesting evaluation; he was offering a feedback system. It is not even necessary for students to put their names on the papers of the weekly quizzes. If students don't believe the teacher is not evaluating them, they can be instructed to leave their names off. The feedback is almost as valuable without names.

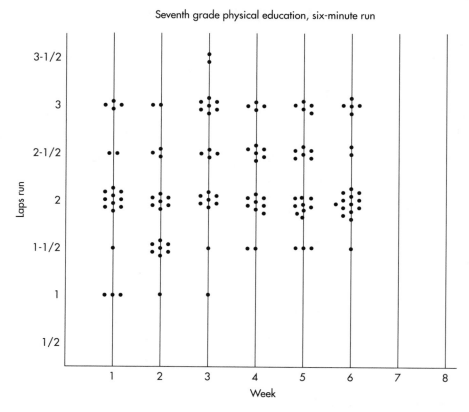

FIGURE 7-13. Class scatter diagram for seventh grade physical education.

Dr. Deming probably said at every seminar he gave that there is no shortage of good people unless we create the shortage. Statistics is a powerful way to create a shortage of good people. Education adopted a terrible term for average: *grade level*. Most people know that 50 percent of the population is above average by any measure and 50 percent is below average. They do not know, however, that *grade level* is a synonym for average. Fifty percent of students are below average, and thus below grade level. America has done great harm to its future by labeling half of its students below grade level. Therefore on the spelling, reading, geography, and physical education graphs in this chapter there is no line for average. As soon as a teacher or administrator decides the graphs can be *improved* by adding an average line, he or she has communicated to 50 percent

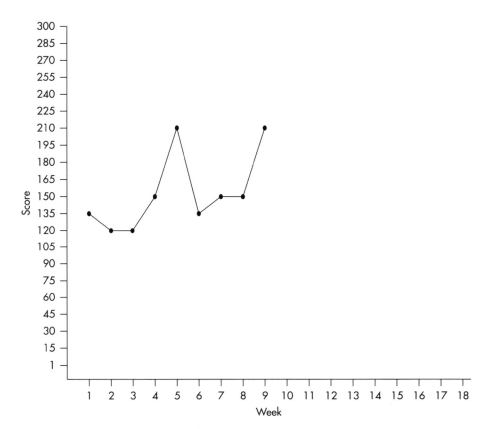

FIGURE 7-14. Class run chart for eighth grade science.

of the pupils that they don't quite have what it takes to be successful. This *average* line is harmful to students all year, but especially so at year's end. For example, if students are tested on 17 spelling words each week, more than half of the students are likely to get 17 correct on the last week of school. Thus, the student with 16 correct would be below average if an average line were constructed. Teachers who are expending great effort to improve quality in their classrooms will want to avoid such a negative message. Instead, the message should be, "I'm proud of you for improving from three to five words correct each week to a final-week score of 16 right."

Critics of Dr. Deming's theories might not appreciate the previous discussion because it seems to take away personal initiative

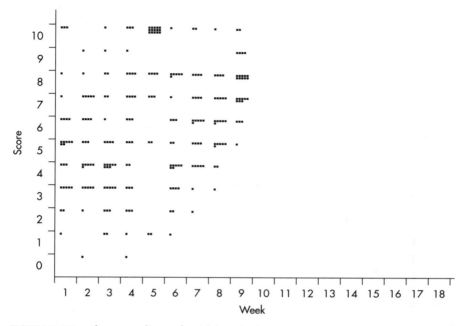

FIGURE 7-15. Class scatter diagram for eighth grade science.

or responsibility for problems. Remember, however, Dr. Deming stated that 94 percent of problems are caused by the system.[6] He didn't say that 100 percent of the spelling (or math, geography, or reading) problems in a classroom are caused by the educational system, but rather that 94 percent of those problems are caused by the system. He would not have educators blame the students for the problems, but instead roll up their sleeves, put their heads together, listen to the parents and students, consult with experts, and fix the 94 percent of the problems for which they are responsible. In his words, "Quality comes not from inspection, but from improvement of the production process."[7]

I mentioned in the book's preface a graph a teacher, Karen Fauss, showed me indicating that the 1995–96 class was, in March, already ahead of the prior year's class. Figure 7-16 shows the class spelling run chart that provides the teacher with this feedback. In weeks 20 and 26 the class matched the prior class's top spelling score, which occurred in week 35 (see Figure 7-1). The credit for this improvement could lie with the first grade teachers, as the class started out second grade at a higher level; or the credit might be due the second grade teacher. It matters not. The spelling

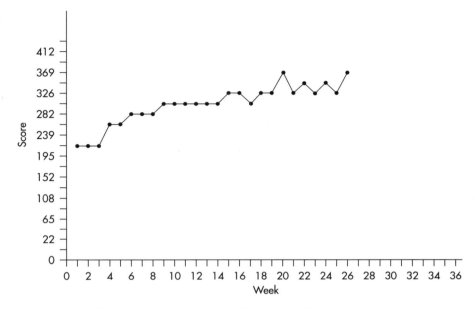

FIGURE 7-16. Class run chart for second grade spelling, March 1996.

system seems to have improved, everyone contributed, and everyone can celebrate. Quality was not achieved by inspection, but by improvement of the spelling production process.

Notes

1. W. Edwards Deming, *Out of the Crisis* (Cambridge, Mass.: MIT Press, 1986), p. 14.
2. The 100-sided die, "Zocchihedron," is a product of Gamescience in Gulfport, Miss.
3. Kevin Jenkins, as quoted by Karen Bemowski in "Leaders on Leadership," *Quality Progress* 29(1): 45.
4. W. Edwards Deming, American Association of School Administrators Conference, Washington, D.C., January 1992.
5. W. Edwards Deming, *Schools and Communities Cooperating for Quality—Lessons for Leaders* (seminar sponsored by American Association of School Administrators, Alexandria, Va., 1990, handout), ch. 6, p. 8.
6. W. Edwards Deming, *The New Economics* (Cambridge, Mass.: MIT Press, 1993).
7. Deming, *Out of the Crisis.*

Chapter 8
MEASURING KNOWLEDGE

Measuring information as described in Chapter 7 is analogous to measuring at a track-and-field event. The questions *how far, how high,* and *how fast* are simple and can be answered by counting. Little judgment is needed and machines can do some of the counting. Measuring information is the same; the scoring requires little judgment and a machine can do much of the counting.

Measuring growth in knowledge, however, is analogous to measuring at a gymnastics event. There is only one question, but it is not as simple: "On a 1-to-10 scale, how well did the gymnast perform?" Much judgment is needed, and machines are not qualified to score. Measuring knowledge is the same; scoring requires talented, highly trained judges.

Critics of performance-based assessment say such test results are not accurate because they are subjective. Judging quality is subjective, but that does not make it inaccurate. The first purpose of this chapter is to outline steps necessary for public confidence in measuring knowledge. The second purpose is to demonstrate the use of statistical tools for measuring knowledge.

A continuum of quality from lowest levels to highest levels is necessary for measuring knowledge. Reading ability, for example, can be described in 10 levels. Level 1 is the ability to read letters of the alphabet, one's own name, and well-known symbols, plus knowing that English print is read from left to right. Level 10 is the reading skill required of students in high school advanced-placement English classes.

Levels 1 through 6 are used to describe the typical growth of elementary students; levels 7 and 8 describe the levels of accomplishment achieved by middle school students; and level 9 describes the expected achievement in grade 12. Those who create such scales must first agree on a precise aim for the subject and then use their collective knowledge to build each step of the continuum.

The reason for recommending a 1-to-10 scale is California state assessment experience. A 1-to-6 scale for grade four, a more difficult 1-to-6 scale for grade eight, and an even more difficult 1-to-6 scale for grade 10 are troublesome to explain to the public. A student making normal progress in grade four would score a 4 in grade four, a 4 in grade eight and another 4 in grade 10. People close to educational assessment understand, but to many members of the public this seems confusing.

The major disadvantage of a 1-to-10 scale seems to be its inability to show growth throughout a school year. A score that serves well for end-of-the-year summative data is not precise enough for the small, incremental growth that occurs from month to month. I predict that if America accepted the 1-to-10 scale as a norm and if many people in various parts of the United States published their scales, in time the scales would appear with decimals. These smaller increments could then be used to measure growth throughout the school year.

Figures 8-1 through 8-5 show the results of five years of measuring all fourth grade students within a school district on writing,

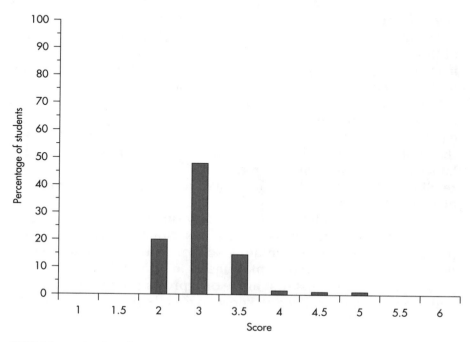

FIGURE 8-1. Fourth grade writing histogram, 1992.

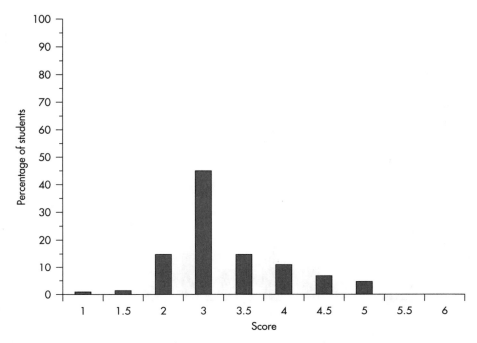

FIGURE 8-2. Fourth grade writing histogram, 1993.

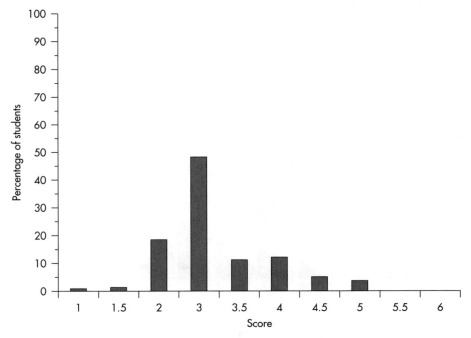

FIGURE 8-3. Fourth grade writing histogram, 1994.

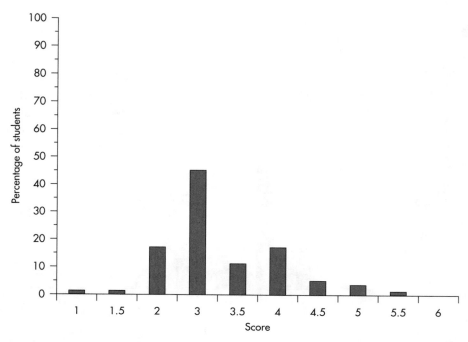

FIGURE 8-4. Fourth grade writing histogram, 1995.

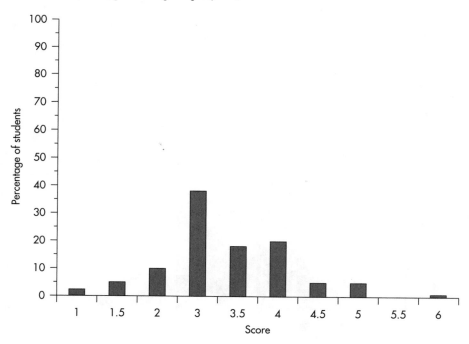

FIGURE 8-5. Fourth grade writing histogram, 1996.

using a 1-to-6 scale. Teachers met together one day a year to score student writing. Each student paper was read by two teachers other than the teacher who assigned the writing. If the two scores were identical, the number was recorded. If the scores were different by only one point, the score was recorded as an average of the two. This explains the half-point scores on the graphs. If the two scores differed by more than one point, a third teacher was brought in to help reach consensus.

Knowledge is also measured throughout the school year using run charts and scatter diagrams. Experiments have been conducted documenting growth in mathematical problem solving. Students were provided one open-ended problem to solve each month. The answer was scored on a 1-to-6 scale. In a class of 30 pupils, a perfect month would have been a score of 180, with all students scoring a 6. Other than the fact that the scale is from 1 to 6 instead of from 0 to 14, the graphs for mathematical problem solving (knowledge) and the graphs for spelling (information) are identical. The first resource that will be used for mathematics knowledge assessment is *How to Evaluate Progress in Problem Solving,* a 1987 publication from the National Council of Teachers of Mathematics. Appendix C shows the publication's Analytic Scoring Guide, a significant contribution to the measurement of knowledge. The second resource is *Measuring Up* from the Mathematical Sciences Education Board. The council's recommendation for a five-point scale is also shown in Appendix C.

Figures 8-6 and 8-7 are graphs from a seventh grade English class measuring writing. The run chart and scatter diagram again document that Dr. Deming's concepts regarding educational statistics work equally well for information and knowledge. Even when a teacher only measures on a rubric three times a year, the data are far more meaningful than data received in July after the students have matriculated to the next grade level. An example of this is shown in Figures 8-8 and 8-9, from a third grade classroom.

The same teacher who provided the science data in Chapter 7 experimented with collecting science knowledge on an 8-point continuum (see Appendix B) in a different science class. The resulting class run chart and class scatter diagram are shown in Figures 8-10 and 8-11. Even though only four sets of data was collected over a nine-week period, it is obvious that improvement has begun.

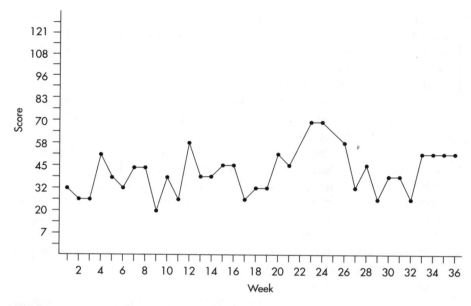

FIGURE 8-6. Seventh grade writing class run chart.

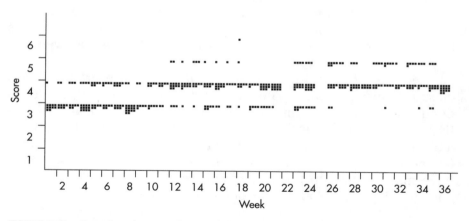

FIGURE 8-7. Seventh grade writing class scatter diagram.

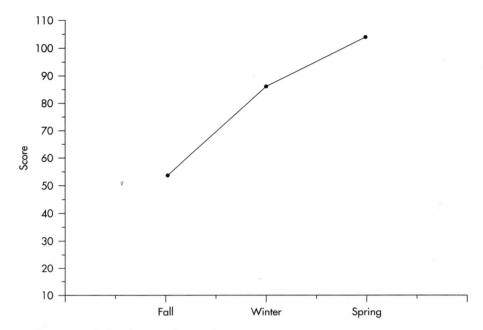

FIGURE 8-8. Third grade writing class run chart.

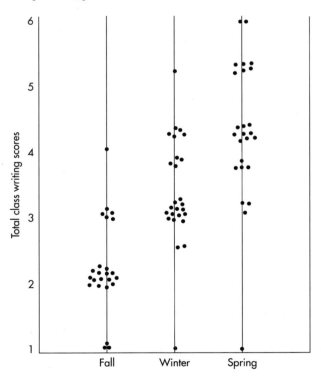

FIGURE 8-9. Third grade writing class scatter diagram.

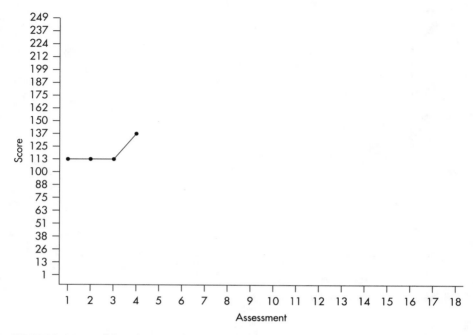

FIGURE 8-10. Eighth grade science class run chart.

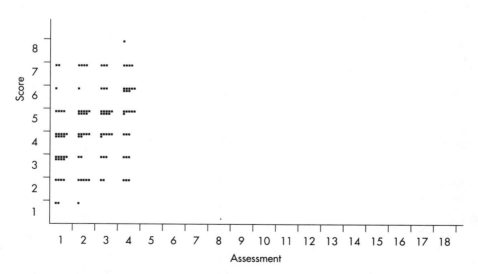

FIGURE 8-11. Eighth grade science class scatter diagram.

Quality measurement of knowledge involves (1) stating course expectations; (2) developing rubrics for single events and continuums to measure quality of work over time; (3) assessing students regularly; (4) organizing the assessment data into a classroom run chart and a classroom scatter diagram; and (5) regularly using the feedback to make course corrections so all can be successful.

Chapter 9
CLASSROOM IMPROVEMENT

An annual responsibility for teachers is to document classroom production. Figure 9-1 displays, for example, the spelling scores of a second grade class at year's end. Of 98 total words given on weekly tests (14 words per week for seven weeks), the class produced eight students who made five or fewer errors, four who made between six and 10 errors, and so on.

The purpose of the year-end histogram is to have baseline data for the next year's improvement. What can be improved next year to produce better spellers? Instead of assuming that next year's class will have better or worse spellers based on good or bad luck,

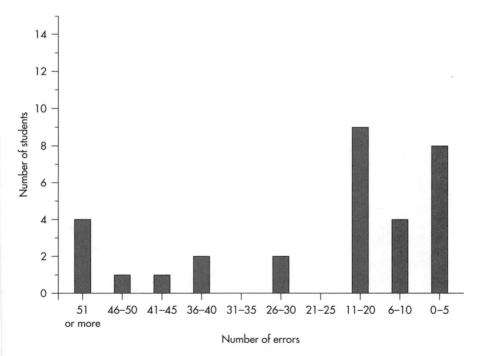

FIGURE 9-1. Second grade spelling histogram, 1995, at year's end.

a teacher who accepts Dr. Deming's thinking believes each year's students can improve over prior years' students. Improvement means less failure at the left of the histogram and more success at the right of the histogram. Figure 9-2 includes the scores of the second grade classroom one year later for comparison.

Class run charts, student run charts, and class scatter diagrams are all feedback to students and teachers so that the final histogram at the end of the year is not a surprise. Quality is built into the system through regular feedback and adjustment instead of inspected in at the end.

Four other examples of end-of-year class histograms are shown in Figures 9-3 through 9-6.

Figure 9-3 shows students' scores for math concepts. The average of the last two months measured on a mid-year assessment

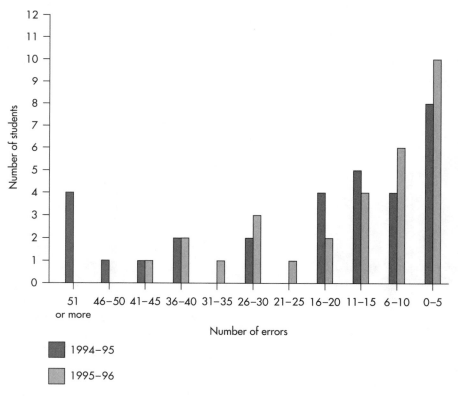

FIGURE 9-2. Second grade spelling histogram comparing 1995 and 1996.

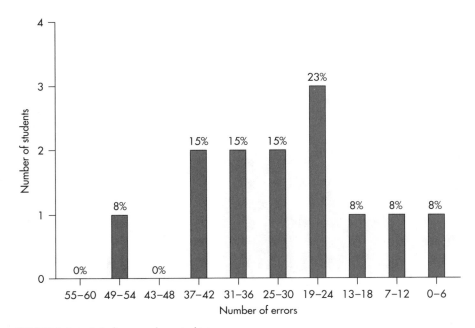

FIGURE 9-3. End-of-year mathematics histogram.

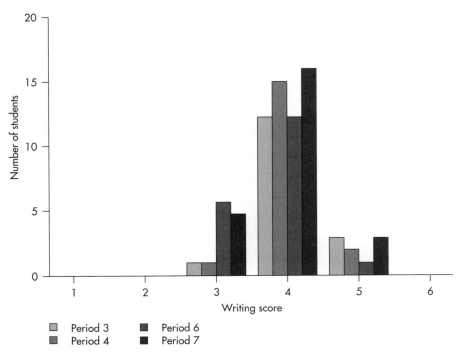

FIGURE 9-4. End-of-year writing histogram.

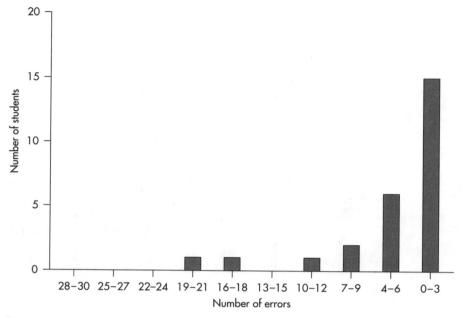

FIGURE 9-5.   End-of-year geography histogram.

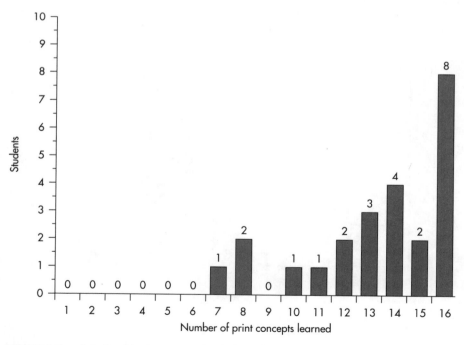

FIGURE 9-6.   End-of-year kindergarten reading histogram.

is designed to assist a teacher in improving student learning before year's end.

Figure 9-4 shows students' writing scores on a 1-to-6 rubric. The end-of-year histogram displays the average of the last two months.

Figure 9-5 shows geography scores from fifth graders quizzed on 200 world locations. Thirty of the 200 locations were randomly selected for the test to determine end-of-year production.

Sixteen indicators of kindergartners' future reading success are listed in Table 9-1; these indicators were measured to determine the scores shown in Figure 9-6. The histogram displays the number of students who demonstrated their knowledge of the reading success indicators.

Figure 9-7 is a histogram for seventh grade spelling. Students were quizzed each week on 32 spelling words randomly selected from a list of 1000. The histogram shows the total errors for the last four weeks of the year. Figure 9-8 is a histogram for fifth grade spelling. Teachers gave four 25-word quizzes in May. The words are randomly selected from a list of 500.

An example of a science class histogram is shown in Figure 9-9. It documents the number of errors on the school year's last three 10-item quizzes. The stage is now set to see if next year's class can outperform this year's class.

Once a clear aim is selected for a particular subject and the results of last year are known, the improvement process starts again. What methods, materials, equipment, people, and learning environment changes can be made that will possibly result in actual improvement? Dr. Deming would have teachers plan out a strategy, study initial results, and, if positive results occur, work the experiment into normal classroom operation. The plan-do-study-act cycle then starts over. Classroom scatter diagrams and classroom run charts allow teachers to regularly check the results of improvement experiments and continually build in more quality.

A caution should be added, however, on making changes too rapidly. If a teacher changes the teaching strategy after each assessment, this is tampering, much like a legislature operates. The experiment must be carried out for a reasonable period of time before a teacher knows whether the results (either good or bad) are the result of luck or improvement. *Reasonable period of time* has been fairly well defined by statisticians.

TABLE 9-1.   Assessment for kindergarten language arts: Concepts-about-print checklist.

Teacher's name: _____   School: _____   Date: _____

	Teacher questions	✔	Concept
•	***Before reading, ask the child:***		
1.	Where is the front of the book?		Book concepts—front cover
2.	Can you point to the title?		Book concepts—title
3.	Where do we start reading?		Reading concepts—print carries the message
4.	Which way do we go when we're reading?		Directionality—left to right in a sentence
5.	Where do we go when we get to the end of the line?		Directionality—return sweep
•	***During reading, ask yourself:***		
6.	As the child reads and points to the text, is there an exact match between the number of words spoken and the number of words printed?		Reading concepts—one-to-one correspondence
•	***After reading, ask the child:***		
7.	Can you put your fingers around a word?		Word concept
8.	Can you put your fingers around a letter?		Letter concept
9.	Can you find a capital letter?		Capital letter
10.	Can you find a small letter?		Small letter
•	***Writing and listening:***		
11.	Uses letters in writing		Letters represent words
12.	Writes own first name		Recognition of own name
13.	Writes five or more words correctly		Use of standard spelling
14.	Listens to and recites familiar rhymes; sings familiar songs		Memory skills/sequencing
•	***Beginning Reading***		
15.	Can you find 10 words you can read?		Reads 10 words
16.	Ask student sounds and letter names one at a time		Names and knows sounds of 20 letters

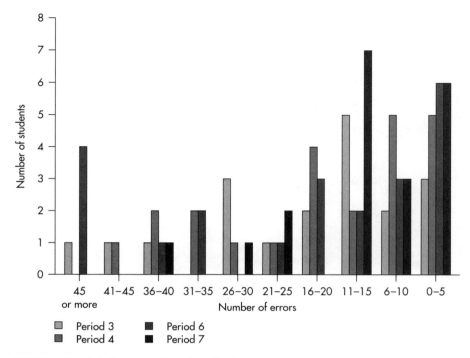

FIGURE 9-7. End-of-year seventh grade spelling histogram.

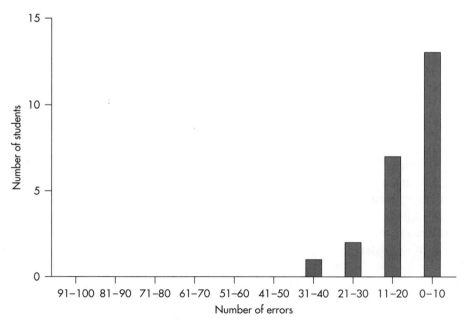

FIGURE 9-8. End-of-year fifth grade spelling histogram.

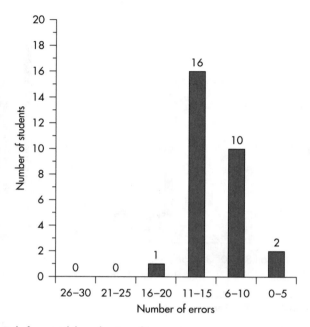

FIGURE 9-9. End-of-year eighth grade science histogram.

If a class improved the first week into an experiment, there is a 50 percent chance the students were lucky and a 50 percent chance they improved. On a spelling quiz with randomly selected words, luck would mean easy or known words came up randomly. On a writing assignment, luck would mean the assigned topic matched the experiences of many students and thus they were able to write better. This 50-50 chance is the same as flipping one coin and having it come up heads.

If the class improves the second week, the students now have a 25 percent chance they were lucky and a 75 percent chance they actually improved. This is the same 25-75 chance of flipping two coins and having both come up heads. If the class again improves the third week, the chance of luck is 12.5 percent and the chance of improvement is 87.5 percent. This is the same 12.5-87.5 chance of flipping three coins and having three heads come up. Table 9-2 shows the luck-improvement ratios from 50 percent luck down to less than 1 percent luck.

Conservative statisticians say that seven weeks of collecting data after a change has been made is necessary to prove whether

TABLE 9-2. Luck improvement ratios.

Weeks	Percent chance luck	Percent chance improvement
1	50%	50%
2	25%	75%
3	12.5%	88.5%
4	6.25%	93.75%
5	3.1%	96.9%
6	1.6%	98.4%
7	0.8%	99.2%

the growth is due to luck or improvement. Why seven weeks? Because statisticians want to be able to say there is less than a 1 percent chance the growth was caused by good luck. It seems reasonable to accept this advice when students are quizzed once a week in a particular subject. When monthly quizzes are given, however, four months of consistent growth should rule out good luck as the reason for the improvement.

Teachers will naturally balk at this amount of record keeping and graphing. Their day is already long, and they don't have secretaries. With computer programs,[1] however, the graphs can be produced without spending extra time. The screen display looks exactly like a traditional grade book, with names and cells for scores. As long as the teacher enters the scores directly into the computer, instead of recording them elsewhere and then later transferring them to a computer, no additional time is required. The input is identical; the data for teacher decision making is, however, light-years ahead in terms of quality.

Classroom improvement is a never-ending process composed of (1) establishing the aim; (2) displaying what is being produced now on a histogram; (3) experimenting with improvement strategies; (4) gathering feedback through run charts and scatter diagrams; (5) placing strategies that work into the culture of the classroom; (6) charting another year-end histogram; and (7) starting over. Teachers need at least two comparative histograms. Figure 9-10 compares the results from a classroom, school, and district. This allows a teacher to better understand improvement needs. The second comparative histogram is Figure 9-11, which displays two successive years. Some might say the

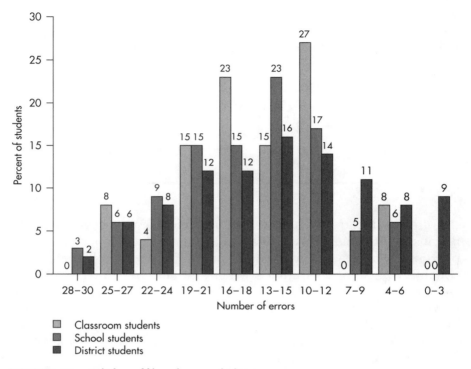

FIGURE 9-10. End-of-year fifth grade geography histogram.

teacher was only lucky in 1995–96; no real improvement occurred. Luck is possible, as discussed earlier in this chapter, but even so, it is human nature to desire the next year to be even better. When exceptional success occurs, the aim of the course is rewritten to a higher standard and the improvement process starts over.

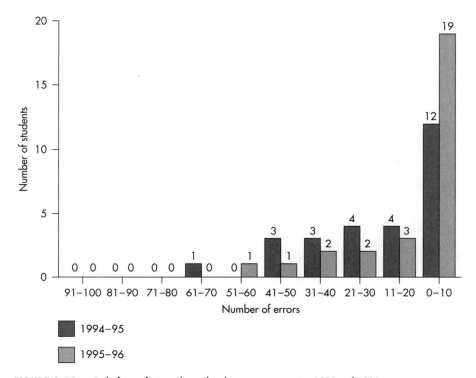

FIGURE 9-11. End-of-year first grade reading histogram comparing 1995 and 1996.

Note

1. *Quality School Measurement* software, Enterprise School District, 1996.

Chapter 10
STUDENT IMPROVEMENT

At one of the many dinners that school superintendents have the privilege of attending, I sat next to a man who had been the victim of an automobile accident. The trailer being towed by the car he was following came loose. It spun around, and the tongue plowed through his car. The result was serious injury, surgery, and many sessions of painful physical therapy.

What did this man in his forties need to help him endure the pain of therapy? He needed feedback from the therapist. Each week his ability to move his arms and legs was measured and the growth in his flexibility was graphed. Observing the graphs, he could see his progress and thus concluded the pain was worthwhile.

Students who are older than third grade and struggling with learning to read are usually in pain. The joyful process of learning to read as a 5-, 6-, 7-, or 8-year-old has been replaced by embarrassment, self-consciousness, and feelings of failure. Such students need weekly feedback to document that growth is occurring and the pain is worth it. When children have no feedback that their reading assignments are producing positive results, they determine that the pain of doing the work is not worthwhile. The 40-year-old injured driver could not determine on his own that increased flexibility was returning to his body. The growth was too minute. Likewise, reading growth is often too minute for the student to notice.

Figures 10-1 through 10-4 document the growth of four special education students in reading. Each week their reading speed was charted. The first 10 weeks' average reading speed is indicated with a line on each figure, serving as baseline data against which future growth can be compared. The weekly process began by selecting a book with an appropriate text, and the student began reading. An adult started a stopwatch when the first word was read and stopped the reading one minute later. Any unknown words were pronounced for the student, tallied, and subtracted from the final word-per-minute (WPM) score.

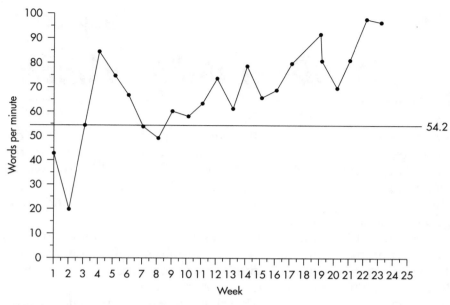

FIGURE 10-1. Special education reading, Student 1.

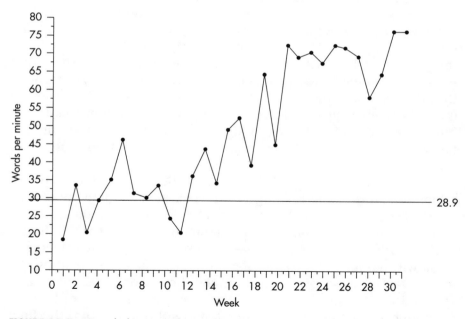

FIGURE 10-2. Special education reading, Student 2.

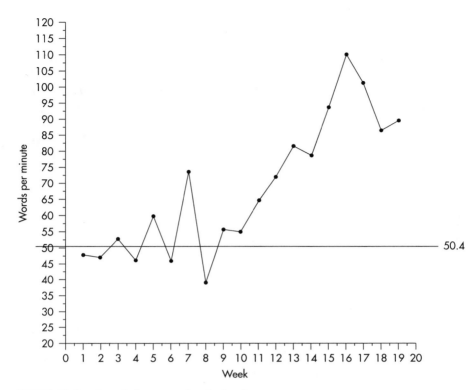

FIGURE 10-3. Special education reading, Student 3.

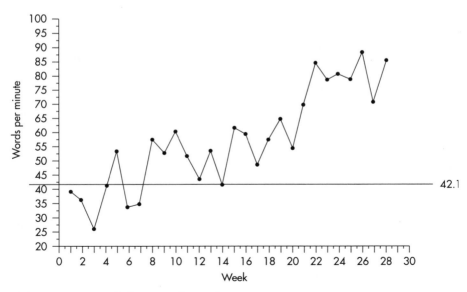

FIGURE 10-4. Special education reading, Student 4.

Growth in any subject can be graphed for individual students. Figures 10-5 through 10-7 are from a fifth grade math class. The students were quizzed each week on 10 out of 100 mathematics concepts.

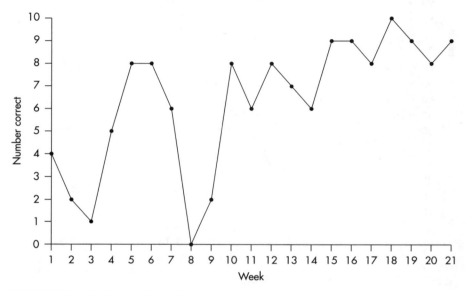

FIGURE 10-5.   Mathematics Student 1.

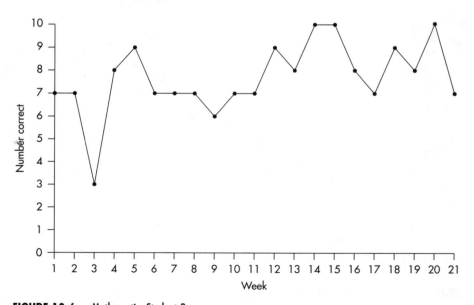

FIGURE 10-6.   Mathematics Student 2.

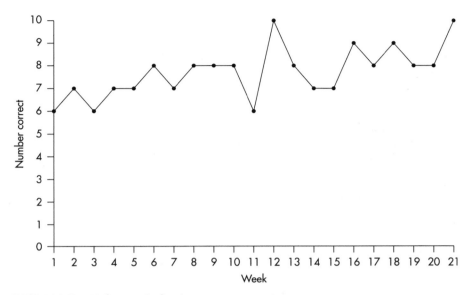

FIGURE 10-7. Mathematics Student 3.

Figures 10-8 through 10-11 are student results in first grade reading. In Chapter 7, the class scatter diagram and run chart for reading were displayed. Figures 10-8 through 10-11 show four of the 30 student run charts from the same classroom.

Student run charts are wonderful parent communicators. Not only do they document growth, which is difficult to communicate through traditional report cards, but they help with concerns about work being too easy, the need for special education, and the frequently asked question, "How is my child doing compared to the rest of the class?"

Figure 10-12 is a run chart of a first grade reader. It is obvious she began the year with a great deal of skill in reading and soon topped out the assessment. As described in Chapter 9, seven weeks of consistent data are needed to rule out luck. Luck in this case would mean that the randomly chosen words the student was asked to read were words in her reading vocabulary, and the words she couldn't read were not selected. For the student in Figure 10-12, it is clear that luck is not a factor. She needs assignments, beyond what is assigned to most, that continually challenge her. (After seven weeks of perfect scores, the student was no longer given the weekly quiz, but the score was entered into the computer to give

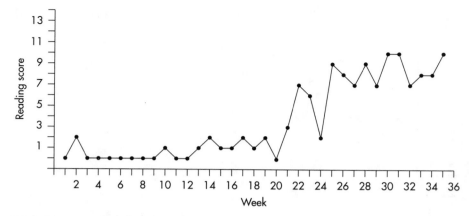

FIGURE 10-8. First grade reading, Student 1.

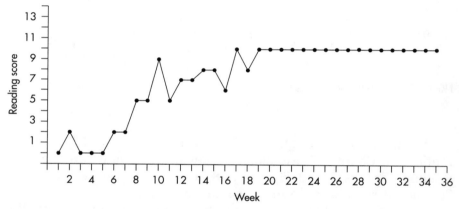

FIGURE 10-9. First grade reading, Student 2.

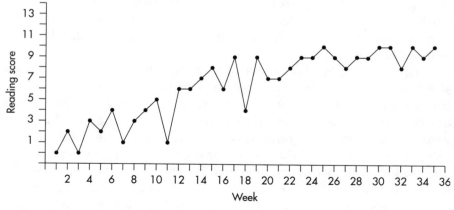

FIGURE 10-10. First grade reading, Student 3.

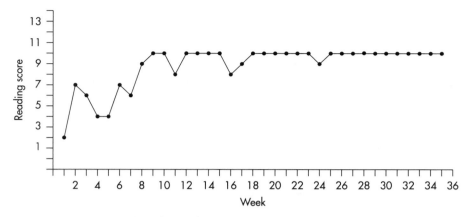

FIGURE 10-11. First grade reading, Student 4.

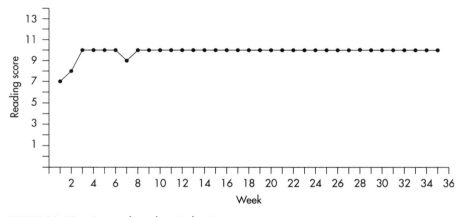

FIGURE 10-12. First grade reading, Student 5.

credit on the class run chart.) Conversely, Figure 10-13 shows that the curriculum is probably appropriate for this particular student.

Figures 10-14 through 10-17 are from second grade spelling. Only four of the run charts from 30 were selected for illustration. If, however, all 30 had been published here, the reader would quickly note that no two graphs are identical. Everyone knows that no two children are alike, but looking at 30 different graphs is a reminder of this fact.

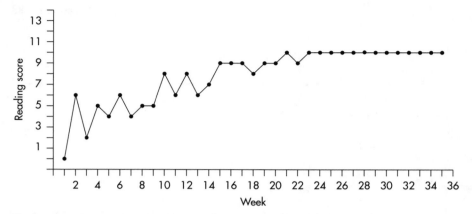

FIGURE 10-13. First grade reading, Student 6.

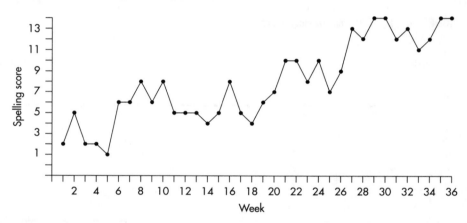

FIGURE 10-14. Spelling Student 1.

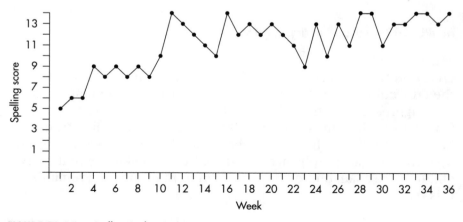

FIGURE 10-15. Spelling Student 2.

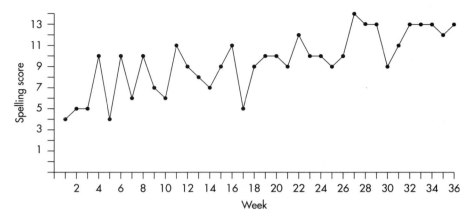

FIGURE 10-16. Spelling Student 3.

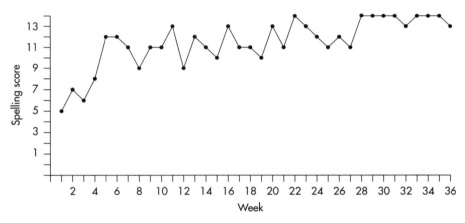

FIGURE 10-17. Spelling Student 4.

Figures 10-18 through 10-20 are from the same student in seventh grade. They show a year's growth in spelling, writing, and reading. The student, a learner of English as a second language (ESL), has every reason to feel proud of his accomplishments.

Dan Flores, an Enterprise District teacher, discovered that overlapping the classroom scatter diagram with a student run chart answers, without ranking, a typical parent question, "How is my child doing compared to the rest of the class?" Figure 10-21 is an example from his classroom. Parents can see the class on the

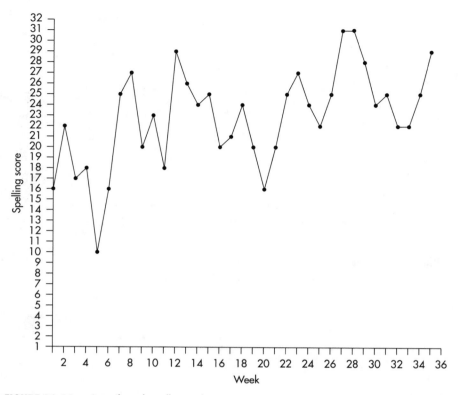

FIGURE 10-18.   Seventh grade spelling student.

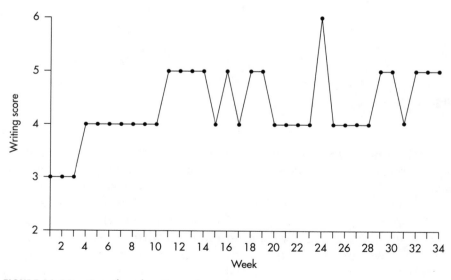

FIGURE 10-19.   Seventh grade writing student.

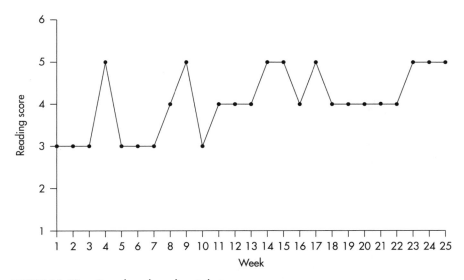

FIGURE 10-20. Seventh grade reading student.

scatter diagram and their child on the run chart. Dan made a transparency of the scatter diagram and a paper printout of each student's run chart. At parent conference time when parents asked this question, he was able to place the transparency over the student's run chart.

The overlaid scatter diagram and student run chart are also useful in making special education decisions. Figures 10-22 through 10-24 are overlaid scatter diagrams and student run charts in reading, writing, and spelling. In the fall, some staff thought this student should receive special education services. Others disagreed. The three charts of up-to-date data supported the viewpoint of one teacher who believed the student did not need special education.

Someday American parents will accept the fact that ranking destroys children's yearning for learning. Parents will trade grades (ranking) for better data. The better data must include (1) clear aims for every subject at graduation; (2) how a particular subject at a particular grade level helps meet the graduation standard; and (3) the progress of each student on the path toward graduation. The information and knowledge student run charts are examples of the data parents desire.

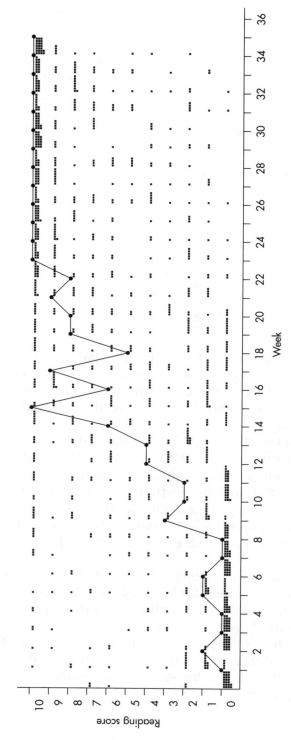

FIGURE 10-21. First grade student reading run chart, overlaid with class scatter diagram.

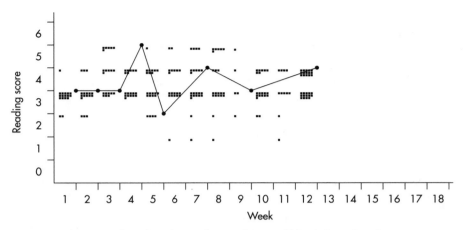

FIGURE 10-22. Seventh grade student reading run chart, overlaid with class scatter diagram.

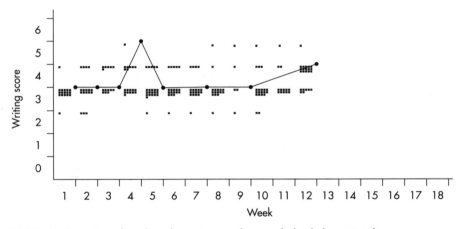

FIGURE 10-23. Seventh grade student writing run chart, overlaid with class scatter diagram.

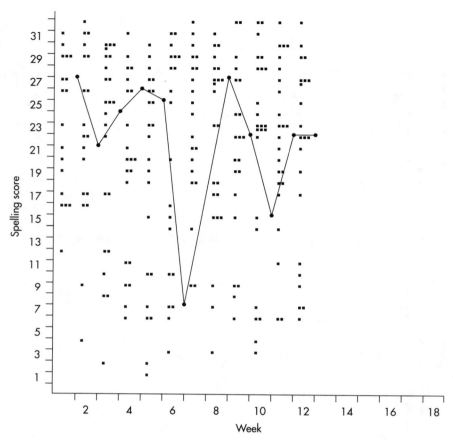

FIGURE 10-24. Seventh grade student spelling run chart, overlaid with class scatter diagram.

Chapter 11
SCHOOL IMPROVEMENT

Surprise. School improvement means less failure and more success. Administrators are responsible for school improvement. Not the teachers. Not the students. Not the parents. The administrators need help from everybody, but they cannot delegate responsibility for quality. Many CEOs in the United States were too important or too busy to attend Dr. Deming's four-day seminar on improving quality, so they sent their assistants to the seminars. This caused him to write, ". . . and if you can't come, send nobody. In other words . . . if you don't have time to do your job, there is not much I can do for you."[1] Again, administrators are responsible for school improvement. If administrators don't have time to do their job, there's not much this book can do for them.

I hope that, by now, those reading this book can write the steps for improvement. The thinking behind improving a classroom and improving a school is almost identical.

First, agree on an aim for each school subject or behavior to be improved. Next, set a standard in both knowledge and information for each subject and each grade level. Note that there is no goal that, say, 90 percent of the students must meet the standard; there is merely a standard. For example,

Knowledge
- Fifth graders write consistently at level 4, 5, or 6 on a six-point scale.
- All students solve grade-level-appropriate mathematics problems at levels 4, 5, or 6 on a six-point rubric.

Information
- Fifth graders spell the 500 most commonly used English words.
- Fifth graders know 200 national, international, and state geography locations.

Behaviors
- Students follow school safety and health rules.
- Students arrive at school on time.
- Students have a good attendance record.
- Third, fourth, and fifth grade students are involved in extracurricular activities.
- Fifth grade students are involved in a leadership project for improvement of the whole school.
- Students maintain enthusiasm for learning.

Principals should then agree, with staff input, on definitions of success and failure for each aim. The actual definitions need to make sense, but since nobody is being ranked or blamed, the definitions aren't crucial. It is expected that all standards will be raised over time. Examples of success and failure include the following:

Standard	Failure	Success
Spelling	Missed 20 or more on 100-word test	Missed 10 or fewer on 100-word test
Writing	Level 1 or 2	Level 4, 5, or 6
Geography	Missed 15 or more on 30-location quiz	Missed 6 or fewer on 30-location quiz
Math problem solving	Level 1 or 2	Level 4, 5, or 6
Behavior	3 or more office referrals in a year	0 or 1 office referral
Punctuality	More than 20 times tardy	Fewer than 5 times tardy
Attendance	More than 20 absences for any reason	Fewer than 11 days absent
Extra curricular activities	None	At least 2 activities
Leadership	None	At least one major responsibility
Enthusiasm	Students with less than 50 percent happy	All happy except 0 or 1 sad or straight face

Figure 11-1 is a recording sheet for actual data from one elementary school. The definitions, number of failures, and percent of successes are written in the empty cells.

Year: 1995–96 _____   School: _____

Data for Web-of-Quality Indicators, K–5

Topic	Number of failures	Percent of success	Number of students in each category
First grade reading F = 31 or more errors S = 10 or less errors	15	81	80
Second grade reading F = 31 or more errors S = 10 or less errors	1	99	57
Third grade reading F = 31 or more errors S = 10 or less errors	2	93	75
Third grade math F = 24 or more errors S = 12 or less errors	14	46	75
Fourth grade math F = 40 or more errors S = 20 or less errors	8	44	67
Fifth grade math F = 40 or more errors S = 20 or less errors	47	8	89
Fourth grade writing F = 1, 2 S = 4, 5, 6	9	18	60
Fifth grade spelling F = 21 or more errors S = 10 or less errors	22	52	89
Fifth grade geography F = 16 or more errors S = 6 or less errors	38	6	89
Enthusiasm F = Students with more than 50 percent sad S = Students who checked all or 1 other than happy	3	26	463
Attendance F = 20+ absences S = 170+ attendance	75	55	463
Discipline F = 3+ office records S = 0, 1 office records	27	94	463
Students in extracurricular activities, Grades 4 and 5 F = none S = participation	22	86	155
Fifth grade leadership F = none S = participation	26	71	89
Tardies F = 5 or more S = 0, 1, or 2 tardies	146	79	463

FIGURE 11-1. School data for web-of-quality indicators.

The data from Figure 11-1 is displayed on success and failure webs. Figures 11-2 and 11-3 display the first two years' data from the same elementary school. The failure web points to zero because the goal is to have no failure. The reason for using actual numbers is to focus staff attention on real people rather than a percentage of failure. Three failures in writing can encourage a staff to work together to reduce failure, whereas 2 percent failure doesn't sound so bad. Second, the blank webs are identical for each school. Each school, no matter what its size, has the same ultimate goal— zero failures. In Stephen Covey's words, the failure web documents success at "starving our problems."[2] The only caution necessary here is best given in Dr. Deming's words: "Performance and style, whatever these words mean in the minds of customer, must show constant improvement. Zero defects is not sufficient."[3] Whenever a school improves to the point that it has no failure in a particular area, the requirements must be raised for continual improvement.

The success web does not use raw data, but percent instead. The goal on the success web is 100 percent success. Each school, no matter what its size, is working toward 100 percent success; it is "feeding opportunities."[4]

The webs allow school communities to see all of the improvement data from each subject or selected behaviors for multiple years. Each year is shown using a different line, which makes improvement more apparent. Space has been left on the webs for future additional standards. The actual webs used in schools are printed in color on 11-by-17-inch paper, and are thus more legible than the smaller, black and white ones included in this book.

Principals receive or build for themselves a complete histogram for each quality indicator. Figure 11-4, for example, shows second grade reading scores for the same school as shown on the web. Principals also need an identical histogram for the entire district to put each school's performance into perspective. Figure 11-5 is such a document for third grade reading. Figure 11-6 is an example of a school histogram related to middle school suspensions. In addition to the advantages described here, such data help the staff and community focus on the fact that 1000 students had no suspensions, instead of thinking about the nine students who had four or more suspensions. Even when histograms like these are provided, the zero column is often overlooked.

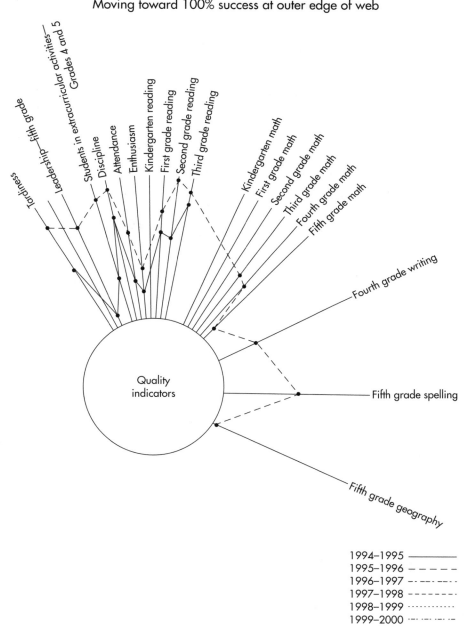

Excellence celebration, K–5:
Moving toward 100% success at outer edge of web

FIGURE 11-2. Celebration-of-excellence web for one school.

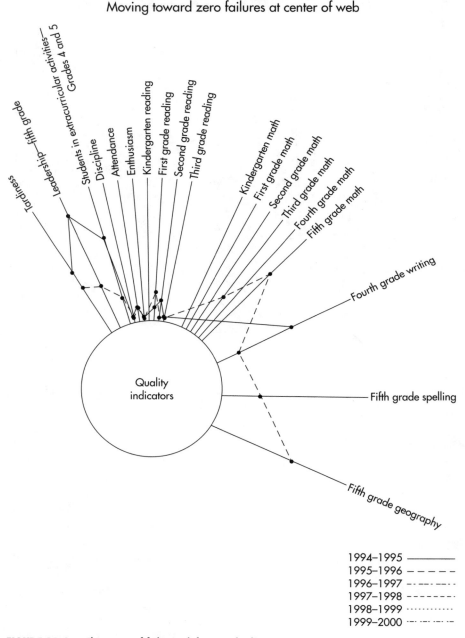

Elimination of failure, K–5:
Moving toward zero failures at center of web

FIGURE 11-3. Elimination-of-failure web for one school.

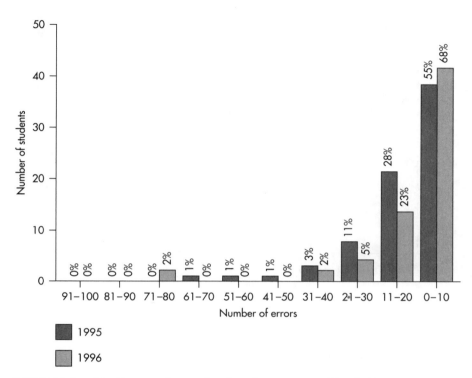

FIGURE 11-4. School histogram for second grade reading comparing 1995 and 1996.

Because numeric goals are an integral part of Western management, it is worth repeating Dr. Deming's 11th point for transformation: "Eliminate numerical quotas."[5] Even though I stated that the ultimate goal was no failure and 100 percent success, this statement is a direction, not a numeric goal. For example, if a school has 10 fifth graders who, at year's end, miss more than 30 of the last 100 spelling words, the improvement goal for next year is to have fewer than 10 failures in spelling. Picking out a numeric goal such as, "Our goal is to have seven or fewer failures next year" is folly. Dr. Deming said numeric goals are plucked out of the sky, with one number being as good as any other. Under a continual improvement philosophy the only goals are less failure and more success. If the school improved from 10 failures to nine the next year, this is improvement. The amount of improvement doesn't matter. Should a school pull the number 8 out of the sky as the goal for failures in

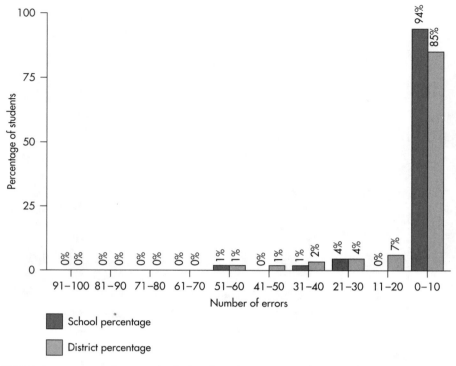

FIGURE 11-5. District histogram for third grade reading comparing school and district.

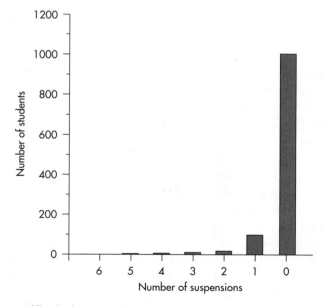

FIGURE 11-6. Middle school suspension histogram.

spelling but produce nine failures, it would not celebrate improvement because it didn't meet its artificial goal. This is tragic.

In addition to improvement on existing radii of the web, schools always have the option of adding a new radius for an additional topic. The process is the same.

1. In what new subject or behavior do we desire improvement?
2. What is the aim?
3. How do we define success and failure?
4. What is the system producing now? Display on a histogram.
5. By what method do we plan to bring about improvement?
6. How will we know our progress throughout the year?
7. Did we improve? (In order to state that improvement has occurred there must be progress on both the success and failure webs. Improvement on one web indicates a redirecting of resources, but not an overall improvement of the organization.)

Webs help leaders work with all parties to devise methods to improve learning. The increase in successes and decrease in failures are celebrated by all.

Residents of Redding, California, enjoy the view of snow-covered Mts. Lassen and Shasta. The mountains have a certain beauty each August when the snow is gone, but after the first fall snow, people are pleased that their two mountains are back in prime condition.

Likewise teachers take great joy in classroom and school growth. They know that they and the students are the mountain. When they also know they are a part of a school and district improvement effort, the happiness is even more apparent. District improvement is the final touch—like the snow on California's beautiful mountain peaks.

Teachers want their superintendents to take their responsibility for instructional improvement seriously. They might have a little trouble with Dr. Deming's statement, "Quality begins in the boardroom,"[6] but they certainly understand how top decisions affect their students, positively or negatively.

Notes

1. W. Edwards Deming, *Out of the Crisis* (Cambridge, Mass.: MIT Press, 1986), p. 14.
2. Stephen Covey, *The Seven Habits of Highly Effective People* (New York: Simon and Schuster, New York, 1989), p. 154.
3. W. Edwards Deming, *Schools and Communities Cooperating for Quality—Lessons for Leaders* (seminar sponsored by American Association of School Administrators, Alexandria, Va., 1990, handout), ch. 1, p. 14.
4. Ibid.
5. Deming, *Out of the Crisis* (Cambridge, Mass.: MIT Press, 1986), pp. 70–76.
6. Ibid.

Chapter 12
DISTRICT IMPROVEMENT

District instructional improvement is less failure and more success in designated areas or overall production. The figures on first grade reading in Chapter 2 are an example of district improvement. Figures 2-4 through 2-8 show less failure and more reading success every year from 1992 to 1995, with no improvement in 1996. The fourth grade writing histograms in Figures 8-1 through 8-5 are another example of improvement. Every area of the curriculum and every measure of student behavior is a candidate for documentation of district improvement.

Overall improvement can be shown on a scale from criminality to advanced placement credit (see Figure 12-1). Again, improvement is less failure and more success. In this case failure is defined as a criminal or dropout and success is a graduate technically prepared for work or academically prepared for the university.

I hesitated to put convicted criminal in the far left column for fear readers would believe I thought schools produced criminals. There are many, many factors involved in students choosing a life of crime, with failure in school being only one. To leave this category off, however, would diminish the success of many teachers, counselors, administrators, and coaches who through dedication, love, and perseverance have saved numerous students from a life in prison.

District improvement commences with a classroom focus. Standards must be established by educators at every grade, with particular focus on transition points at grades five, eight, and 12. No discussion regarding what kinds of standards is necessary. Educators have been bogged down by questions such as, "Are these minimum, average, or gifted standards?" The standards described in this book are none of these. They are merely standards. If writing at level 4 on a 1-to-6 scale by the end of a particular grade is too easy, this will be borne out by the data and educators will raise the standard.

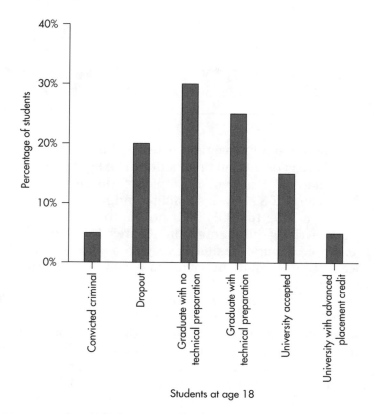

FIGURE 12-1. Hypothetical school district production.

Setting standards is proposing a theory. When educators state that level 4 writing is the standard for fifth grade, this is a theoretical statement to be tested through assessment. The most important advice I can give about standards is to set them *now*. If standards are being used to evaluate individuals, this advice is not good. If, however, data from standards are used as feedback for district improvement efforts, educators must begin now.

Once the standards are selected and agreed on for every school, the district web is created. This web is for the assistant superintendent for instruction; it contains the elements of the school district that all have agreed on and will work together to improve.

It has been my experience that more than 80 percent of a staff need to agree on standards. If a vast majority believe the standards are too low or too high, there will be problems. If they are too low, staff will say the administration wants them that way to look good when the results are published. If they are too high, staff will say administration wants them high to look good in district publications. Therefore, classroom teachers must set the standards, receive the data, and decide when to raise the standards.

As stated in this book's preface, the process of improvement is not top-down, nor is it site based. It is *we* based. Figures 12-2, 12-3, and 12-4 are what *we* agreed. The bilingual staff developed the radius for the English Language Development (ELD) students; fifth grade teachers developed the radius for fifth grade geography and spelling; and seventh grade teachers developed the radius for seventh grade writing. Third grade teachers wrote the third grade mathematics test. They determined that students who scored less than 60 percent correct were failed by the system and students with more than 90 percent correct were successful. The district histogram is shown in Figure 12-5. It is an example of the backup data available for every item on the webs. As more standards are developed by more *we*s, more radii will be added to the webs.

It is possible to implement Dr. Deming's dream to eliminate athletic-type statistics in education. As he would say, "Do it Monday."

Year: 1995–96 _____ School: _____

Data for Web-of-Quality Indicators

Topic	Number of failures	Percent of success	Number of students
First grade reading* F = 31 or more errors S = 10 or less errors	58	72	464
Second grade reading* F = 31 or more errors S = 10 or less errors	38	77	439
Third grade reading* F = 31 or more errors S = 10 or less errors	15	86	428
Fourth grade writing F = 1, 2 S = 4, 5, 6	59	29	382
Seventh grade writing F = 1, 2 S = 4, 5, 6	32	37	322
Enthusiasm F = Students with more than 50 percent sad S = Students who checked all or only 1 other than happy	49	22	3900
Attendance F = 20+ absences S = 170+ attendance	585	44	3900
Discipline F = 3+ office records S = 0, 1 office records	351	89	3900
Spelling, grade 5 F = 21 or more errors S = 10 or less errors	84	59	414
Geography, grade 5 F = 16 or more errors S = 6 or less errors	146	17	414
Math grade 3 F = 24 or more errors S = 12 or less errors 60 questions	108	37	428
Math grade 4 F = 40 or more errors S = 20 or less errors 100 questions	114	31	413
Math grade 5 F = 40 or more errors S = 20 or less errors 100 questions	227	8	414
Title I reading F = no progress S = percent exit	41	20	442
Title I math F = no progress S = percent exit	88	27	403

*Standard was raised for 1995–96.

FIGURE 12-2. School district data for web-of-quality indicators.

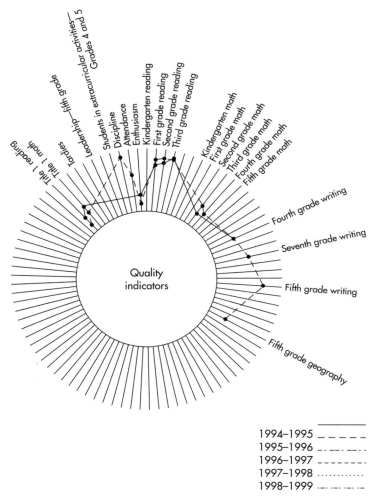

Excellence celebration K–5:
Moving toward 100% success at outer edge of web

Quality indicators

1994–1995	_ _ _ _ _
1995–1996	_ .. _.. _..
1996–1997	_ _ _ _ _ ..
1997–1998	....
1998–1999	_ .. _ .. _ .. _..

FIGURE 12-3.   School district celebration-of-excellence web.

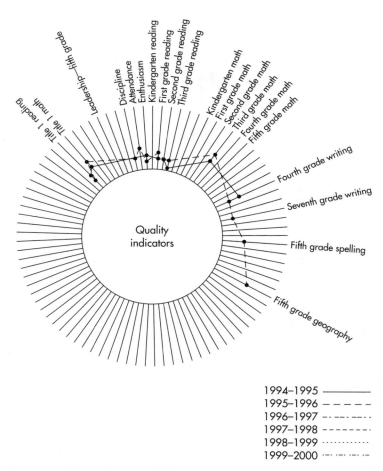

Elimination of failure, K–5:
Moving toward zero failures at center of web

1994–1995 ——————
1995–1996 — — — — —
1996–1997 —·——·——·—·
1997–1998 ——————·
1998–1999 ············
1999–2000 —··——··——··—··

FIGURE 12-4. School district elimination-of-failure web.

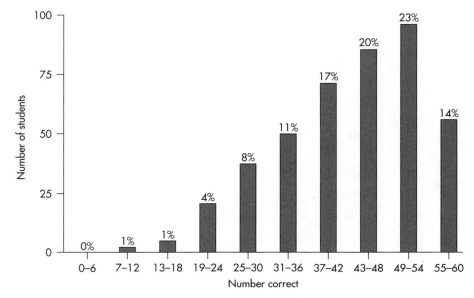

FIGURE 12-5. Third grade mathematics assessment, spring 1996.

Section IV
Enthusiasm Maintained

The prior chapters addressed improved student learning. The next two chapters speak to enthusiasm, learning's twin. What seems more elusive to measure is available for the asking because students freely share their attitudes.

Chapter 13
MEASURING ENTHUSIASM

Children are born motivated to learn. Children enter kindergarten still possessing this enthusiasm for learning. Educators need not motivate children to learn; this was accomplished at birth. The responsibility of educators is to eliminate the loss of innate enthusiasm.

I have heard nobody debate whether children are born motivated to learn. Further, no kindergarten teacher ever told me that children generally lose their yearning for learning prior to beginning school.

I press with the question, "You mean that year after year every student still has enthusiasm at kindergarten's commencement?"

Teachers reply, "Well, it's rare for a kindergartner not to be enthusiastic."

So I probe further. "Maybe one or two students a year start kindergarten with their natural joy for learning gone?"

"Oh no," kindergarten teachers reply. "Maybe one child every five years has had the yearning for learning driven out."

Enthusiasm is not officially considered an asset by educators. Five-year-olds in kindergarten are looked upon as people who have much to learn in the next 13 years. Their educational ledger has many empty pages.

If enthusiasm were considered an asset, educators and other adults would see five-year-olds as having a second ledger completely filled. The children have much knowledge and information to gain, but they have all the enthusiasm they'll ever need. Educators and parents must use all of their collective wisdom to protect this invaluable asset, which is carried around by every kindergartner.

When a new business starts there are also two sets of assets; one is the ideas of the entrepreneur and one is the finances. No matter how great the ideas, when the finances run dry, the business is in serious trouble. In education one start-up asset is the enthusiasm of the students entering our schools. No matter how great the educational opportunities, it is difficult to successfully educate students who have had pages ripped from their enthusiasm ledger.

Enthusiasm can be measured; one needs only to ask the students. Figure 13-1 is a sample questionnaire used by students to communicate enthusiasm. Younger children obviously need more

Fourth Annual Attitude Survey
Enterprise School District
May 1996

Boy ☐ Girl ☐

Grade:

K ☐ 1 ☐ 2 ☐ 3 ☐ 4 ☐ 5 ☐

6 ☐ 7 ☐ 8 ☐

School:

Parsons ☐ Rother ☐ Lassen View ☐

Shasta Meadows ☐ Alta Mesa ☐ Mistletoe ☐

Boulder Creek ☐

FIGURE 13-1. Enterprise School District annual attitude survey.

	 🙂	 😐	 🙁
Reading	☐	☐	☐
Writing	☐	☐	☐
Math	☐	☐	☐
Science	☐	☐	☐
Social studies	☐	☐	☐
Physical education	☐	☐	☐
Health	☐	☐	☐
Music	☐	☐	☐
Art	☐	☐	☐
Drama	☐	☐	☐
Dance	☐	☐	☐
Computers	☐	☐	☐
Spanish	☐	☐	☐

FIGURE 13-1. *Continued.*

explanation and examples, but they readily give opinions. Figure 13-2 charts the data collected over a three-year period. The percentage of happy faces was compiled for each of nine grades, from kindergarten to grade eight.

Educators and the public know that students lose their enthusiasm as they grow older. With no data on when this enthusiasm is lost, it is easy for educators to incorrectly assume when the loss occurs. For example, elementary teachers often assume they keep enthusiasm high and believe secondary educators cause the loss.

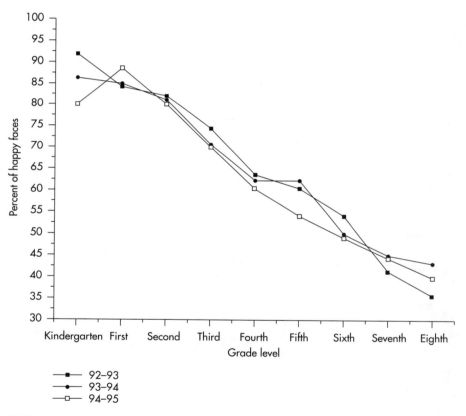

FIGURE 13-2. Enterprise School District 1992–1995 attitude survey results.

The data clearly show that each grade level contributed to the loss of enthusiasm. The loss is gradual, slow, and continual. In simple numbers, if 30 students began kindergarten together, and two students per grade level lost their enthusiasm for learning, only four students would still be enthusiastic after 13 years of schooling. It is a myth that elementary teachers are able to keep enthusiasm high and secondary teachers are unable to match this accomplishment. Dr. Deming must have known about the happy faces when he wrote that Western society continually destroys its people, creating shortages of good people. I'm sure he was baffled at the practice of Silicon Valley executives going outside the United States to hire computer experts. It is not necessary to create shortages of computer expertise, or any other specialized knowledge, in the United States.

A common reaction from educators is, "What *are* we responsible for—learning or enthusiasm?" The answer is both. Because educators are responsible for both learning and enthusiasm, having talented, dedicated, creative teachers in the classroom is crucial. It would be much easier to staff classrooms with teachers who have the attitude of, "You're going to learn whether you like it or not" or "Learning will take care of itself."

Orchestrating classrooms so that all students progress in learning and maintain their enthusiasm for learning is an incredible challenge. It is, however, the responsibility of educators to maintain enthusiasm while increasing learning. We must not allow ourselves to stray from this path.

After seeing the *happy face* data for three years, hearing many discussions on the need for an aim, reviewing Dr. Deming's aim for education, and seeing the kind of learning growth I have described throughout this book, staff of the Enterprise School District wrote and accepted the aim *Maintain enthusiasm while increasing learning.* When the aim was adopted, however, the staff did not know how to accomplish it; but three years of losses in student enthusiasm, convinced them that the future would be no different unless changes were made.

Chapter 14
ANALYZING LOSS OF ENTHUSIASM

Improvement of any aspect of schooling involves several steps. First is the value judgment of an aim. What is the aim of mathematics education? Science education? Education as a whole? Chapter 13 ends with an aim for education, *Maintain enthusiasm while increasing learning.* The second step in the improvement process is gathering data on the current situation. Chapter 13 documents one way to gather information on the loss of learning enthusiasm. The third step is analyzing data, which includes breaking the data into subsets to better understand the system.

Figures 14-1 through 14-9 display the enthusiasm data divided by grade level and subject. Several generalizations can be derived from the charts.

1. The adolescents did not mark their questionnaire with all sad faces. The grownup side of adolescence might cause students to think the questionnaire was beneath them and thus mark everything with a sad face. The sixth, seventh, and eighth graders, however, clearly stated preferences.

2. Changing attitudes is difficult. For example, a slight increase in positive attitude toward social studies occurred between grades five and six. Once students lost their enthusiasm for this particular subject, a talented group of teachers had a great challenge convincing students that their attitude toward social studies was wrong. They had to convince the students that it really is fun to learn about other places and the past.

3. If families and students were the cause for the loss of enthusiasm, then the loss would be consistent from subject to subject.

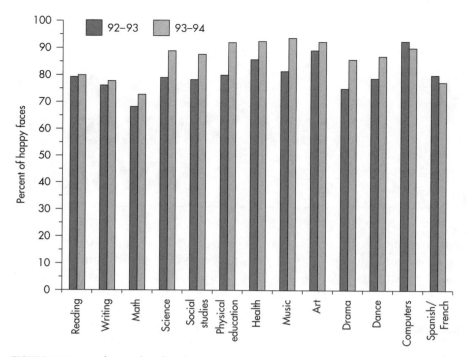

FIGURE 14-1. Enthusiasm by subject for kindergarten.

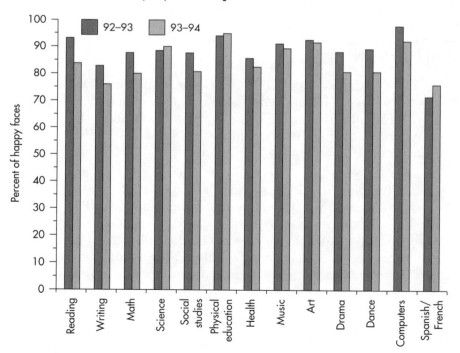

FIGURE 14-2. Enthusiasm by subject for first grade.

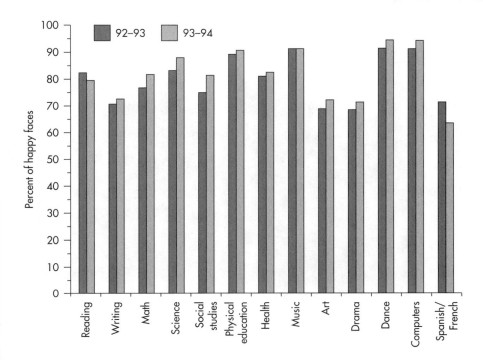

FIGURE 14-3. Enthusiasm by subject for second grade.

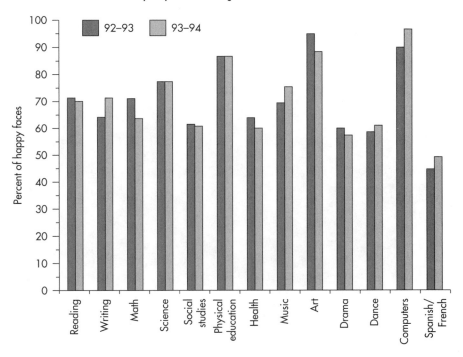

FIGURE 14-4. Enthusiasm by subject for third grade.

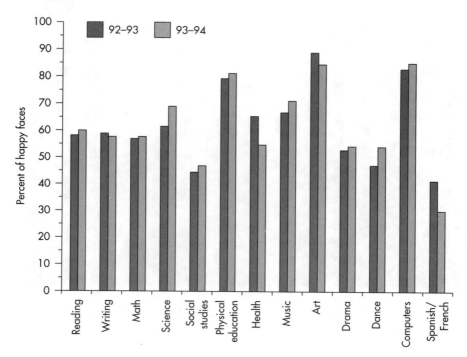

FIGURE 14-5. Enthusiasm by subject for fourth grade.

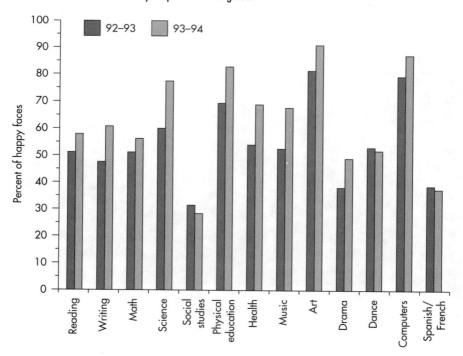

FIGURE 14-6. Enthusiasm by subject for fifth grade.

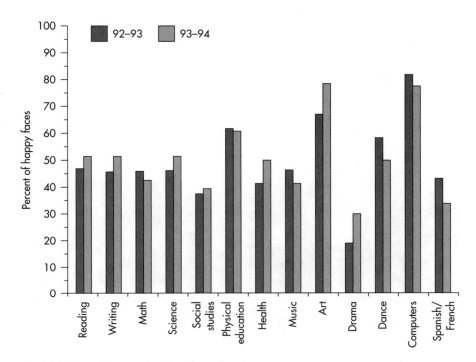

FIGURE 14-7. Enthusiasm by subject for sixth grade.

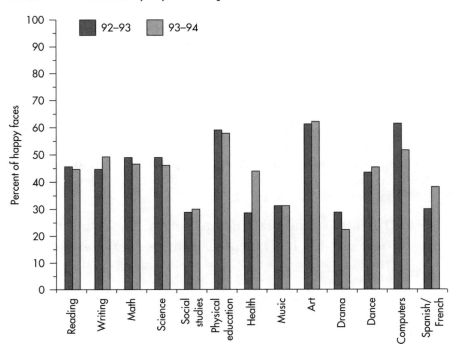

FIGURE 14-8. Enthusiasm by subject for seventh grade.

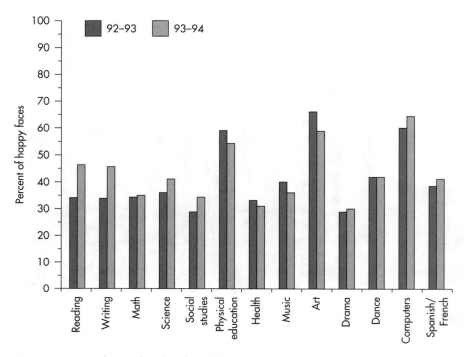

FIGURE 14-9.   Enthusiasm by subject for eighth grade.

4. The students seemed to maintain higher enthusiasm for subjects that had a high rate of hands-on involvement.

The data can also be analyzed by school, subject, and grade level. Figures 14-10 through 14-16 are examples of school enthusiasm graphs for individual schools. By printing each subject in a different color, staff can follow the trend for each subject. Analysis of these data reveals the following:

1. The enthusiasm loss is different from school to school.

2. Some subjects had no enthusiasm loss in the elementary grades of some schools; thus, maintaining enthusiasm is possible.

3. In general, the relative position of a subject remained a constant throughout the middle grades.

4. Improving student enthusiasm is not the norm, but it is possible.

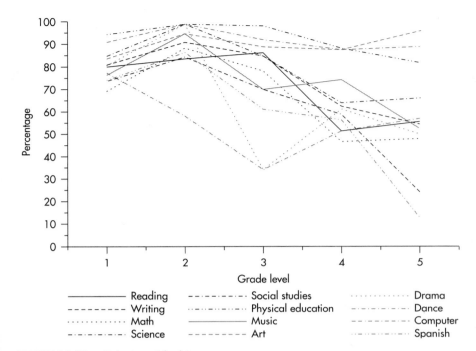

FIGURE 14-10. Enthusiasm, School 1.

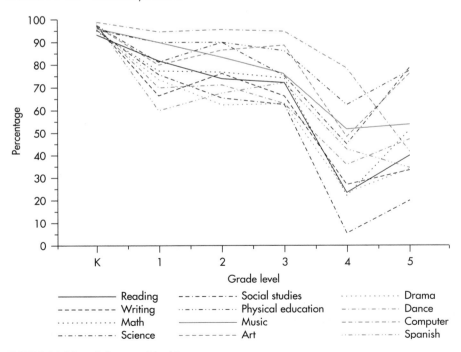

FIGURE 14-11. Enthusiasm, School 2.

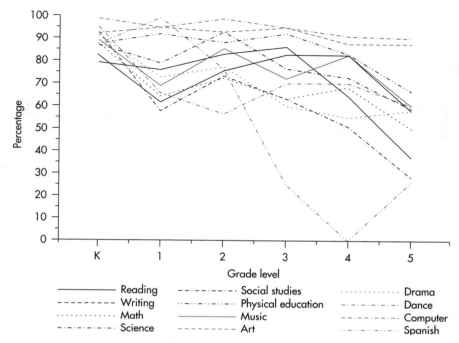

FIGURE 14-12. Enthusiasm, School 3.

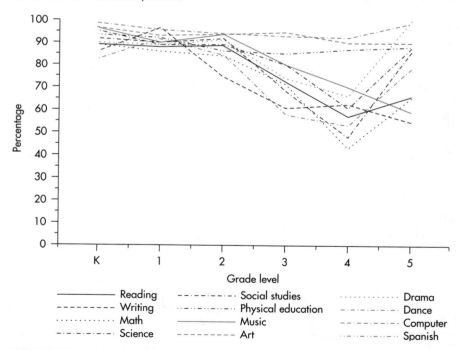

FIGURE 14-13. Enthusiasm, School 4.

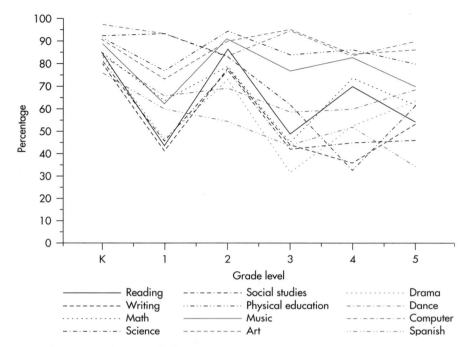

FIGURE 14-14. Enthusiasm, School 5.

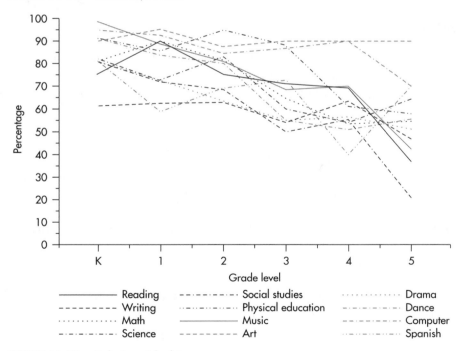

FIGURE 14-15. Enthusiasm, School 6.

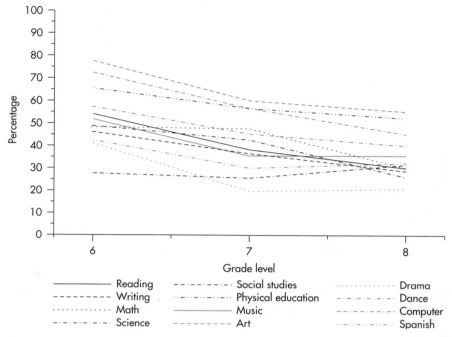

FIGURE 14-16. Enthusiasm, School 7.

5. Enthusiasm has been maintained well for every K–5 subject by at least one sampled school.

6. Some schools had major losses in enthusiasm at particular grade levels.

The maintenance or loss of enthusiasm can be measured, studied, and improved. Enthusiasm loss is a system problem, not an individual teacher or school problem. The loss can only be corrected through teams of students, teachers, parents, board members, and administrators working together. The recipe for working together is Walter Shewhart's plan-do-study-act (PDSA) cycle.

Plan

Planning includes, first of all, determining what the current system is producing overall. Most planning ignores this first step; people rush to do something without a clear grasp of current production. Chapter 13 is an example of defining system production. Because data were gathered over a three-year period, there is no debate that the data truly represent a system.

A second part of planning is further analysis of the current system. The first part of this chapter provides examples of deeper analysis of enthusiasm measurement. The data by school, grade, and subject are a most valuable aspect of planning. It was decided that having male-female analysis would also help with improvement. Figure 14-17 shows enthusiasm loss by male and female for 1996.

A third planning step is the vision. After graphing the current system, the vision is easier to write because the system problems become apparent. The letter that follows is a vision statement that I wrote in 1995. It is a direct result of advice given by Dr. Thomas Harvey, chair of the very successful Department of Educational Management at the University of LaVerne in Southern California. He suggested that the best way to write a vision statement is to project yourself into the future and then write a past-tense marketing letter or brochure describing your organization. So, I wrote a letter to my son and his wife regarding our two grandchildren. It is a vision statement of what I hope for my grandchildren wherever they attend school. (They are three years old and one year old at the time of this writing.) The letter also encompasses much of what I hope for all of the children in schools.

Do

The two subsets of this step are what to do—the decisions—and the actual doing. Section V of this book is devoted to making decisions in general, with a focus on decision making with regard to maintaining enthusiasm.

Study

The next step in the cycle is to study the results. Many means are available for studying results. Here the issue is improvement. Do the results document improvement? Are fewer students losing enthusiasm? In *Improving Student Learning* the web and run chart are selected for the study of experiments conducted under the *do* step of PDSA. The district run chart, the school district web, and the individual school webs are provided in Chapters 11 and 12.

July 1, 1999

Mr. and Mrs. Todd Jenkins
Emeryville, CA

Dear Mr. and Mrs. Jenkins:

Thank you for your recent inquiry regarding our school district. We certainly hope you are able to find the house you desire to purchase within our district boundaries. If not, the choice of where to send Jasmine and Ezekiel is still yours; the staff of Enterprise School District hope you will select us for your children's education. This letter and the enclosed brochures are provided to give you succinct reasons for selecting our school district.

Probably the most important reason for trusting us with Jasmine's and Zeke's education is the high level of student enthusiasm for learning. As you know the brain learns as easily as the lungs breathe. We know cigarettes are a destroyer of lung capacity. Bad attitudes are the equivalent destroyer of brain capacity. The brain will learn what is expected of it unless the innate love of learning given to every child at birth is destroyed.[1]

I know that when you visit our schools and spend time in the kindergartens and first grades, you'll be impressed. The talented, organized staff will convince you that Jasmine and Zeke will be in good hands when they reach school age. But please, don't stop at these visits. Visit all of our sites for middle school and high school education. Here you will observe the same levels of enthusiasm for learning that you saw in kindergarten and first grade.

Both of you know from your own youth that students gradually lose interest in education until, by the end of 12th grade, very few care about learning. When you observe through your visits that a kindergarten level of enthusiasm is maintained at all grade levels, you'll know our schools are the place for Jasmine and Ezekiel.

The enclosed brochures document the learning achievement of our students. Their accomplishments are remarkable. We believe student success is a direct result of implementation of our district aim, *"Maintain enthusiasm while increasing learning."*

Again, thanks for writing; let me know if I can be of further help.

Sincerely,

Superintendent Grandpa

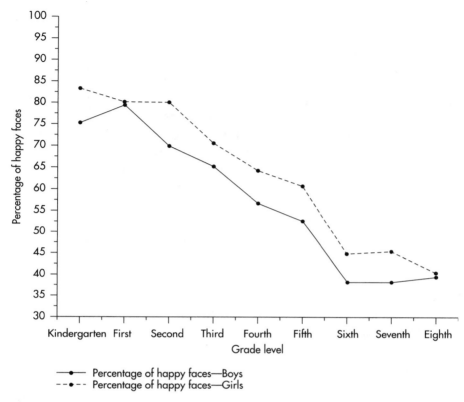

——— Percentage of happy faces—Boys
--•-- Percentage of happy faces—Girls

FIGURE 14-17. Enthusiasm loss by male and female.

It is important for staffs using the PDSA cycle to communicate with each other that not all experiments will result in reduced loss of enthusiasm. Much learning comes from each attempt to bring about improvement.

Act

For those actions that do bring about improvement, *act* is the step to build the experiment into a cultural norm. The successful experiment of the *do* step needs to become *the way we do things around here*. In most organizations this will never happen unless the first three steps are followed consistently. A debate over the validity of the planning data can sabotage changing norms. If the *do* step does not involve decision-making tools, it can become a top-down decision resisted by most. If the *study* step doesn't involve all or most of an organization, then *act* cannot occur because skeptics won't believe the results.

The final part of the *act* step is to start over. After the positive results from *study* have become a part of organizational operation, more improvement is possible. Shewhart wrote a planning cycle in a never-ending circle; he did not write a continuum with an ending.

The loss of enthusiasm by students is a crucial educational issue and a major problem to overcome; all of the intelligence of the quality movement is needed to resolve the issue.

In summary, the PDSA cycle has the following steps.

Plan

1. Determine current system production.
2. Analyze data for causes of poor production results.
3. Envision improvement.

Do

4. Decide which improvement theory to attempt.
5. Implement theory.

Study

6. Study results of experiment.

Act

7. Establish the changes, which resulted in improvement, as organizational norms.
8. Start over.

Note

1. Carl Upchurch, Executive Director of the National Council for Urban Peace and Justice, November 10, 1995, stated at the NCI Symposium in Tampa, Florida, "My crushed spirit didn't allow the brain to breathe."

Section V

Decision Making for Improved Student Learning

Teachers make decisions constantly. Maybe the best synonym for teacher is decision maker, because this seems to be the norm—minute by minute. Section V is devoted to improving the decision-making process so that students learn more and retain their enthusiasm. The decision-making process is described in Chapter 15; ranking, as a decision-making tool, is exposed as harmful in Chapter 16; and the following four chapters describe quality decision-making tools with classroom examples.

Listening is a key component of quality management. Most understand that better decisions are made when education leaders listen to staff, parents, and the community. Each of the decision-making tools described in this section is appropriate for listening to these three groups. The explanations and examples demonstrate how to use each of the four tools.

The examples in Section V, however, do not come from these three traditional sources. I have relied on a fourth source, the students. What do they have to say about ways to improve learning, behavior, enthusiasm, or schooling in general?

Chapter 15
STEPS FOR CLASSROOM IMPROVEMENT

Fifteen steps for improved student learning are delineated under the outline of the PDSA cycle. This may seem like too many steps, but most have already been described in prior chapters. The complete improvement picture is laid out here so that the decision-making process, especially that which involves student input, can be placed in proper perspective.

Plan
Step 1. Establish an aim for the system. See Chapters 1 and 3.

Step 2. Establish an aim for each subject. Students appreciate knowing why they need to know the content of each academic discipline. It is sometimes helpful to begin an aim with the phrase, "to equip students to help others by becoming knowledgeable in [the main ideas of the subject]." Students must realize that expertise in any academic field provides great opportunity to help others.

Step 3. Establish standards for each subject in both information and knowledge. See Chapter 4.

Step 4. Document the present condition for each subject. See Chapter 9.

Step 5. Establish the process for weekly and monthly data collection. See Chapters 7 and 8.

Do
Step 6. Decide on methods of teaching to achieve standards. There are thousands of sources on better methods for teaching each and every subject; it is not, however, the purpose of this book to describe teaching methods.

Step 7. Teach and do whatever else is necessary to help students learn.

Study

Step 8. Review data from the processes established in step 5.

Step 9. Listen to the students through normal questioning, class meetings, and data collected using the quality tools described in this section.

Step 10. Revise teaching methods. Many of the ideas for revisions will come from the students, just like the most successful businesses garner many of their improvement ideas from their customers.

Step 11. Repeat steps 6 through 10. This can be done more often during the school year for information standards than for knowledge standards.

Step 12. Gather end-of-year data on learning and enthusiasm.

Act

Step 13. Build successful teaching revisions into the structure of normal operations.

Step 14. Review aims for possible improvement.

Step 15. Determine that next year, using quality methods, will be better than any prior year. Start over with step 4, which is the data from step 12 of last year.

The PDSA cycle is critical for school districts determined to improve. An improvement-oriented school district that uses the PDSA cycle has few personnel problems, wastes little time on blaming, and focuses on making the future better for children.

Chapter 16

THE WORST EDUCATIONAL DECISION-MAKING TOOL—RANKING

"Abolish ranking. Ranking is a farce. Apparent performance is actually attributable mostly to the system, not to the individual."[1]

Americans spend uncountable sums ranking education: Grade point averages, awards by the thousands, valedictorians, SAT scores on huge scoreboards, dropout rates, and front-page newspaper coverage of school district test scores are all used as the basis for decision making. All communicate who is on top and who (or how many) are on the bottom. Stories in May begin, "Suzan W., daughter of prominent dentist Dr. Harry W., has been selected valedictorian of Cambridge High School." Headlines in June read, "Dropout Rate Reported at 6.2% for County Schools." Such articles explain that this year's dropout rate is better than last year's 6.3 percent rate but worse than the 6.1 percent state average.

None of these data contains any information about improvement. Even comparing this year's dropout rate to last year's is meaningless. Dr. Deming often said the only thing we know for certain about tomorrow's weather is it will be either colder or warmer than today. Similarly, the only thing we know for certain about next year's dropout rate is it will be either better or worse. Having only two data points is worthless *unless* they are used as baseline data to determine if improvement is occurring. Nevertheless, Americans constantly use one or two data points for decision making.

I have chosen to focus on SAT scores in a book written for classroom improvement for two reasons. First, teachers have been criticized in the press over SAT scores and appreciate a rational, apolitical look at the data. Second, it is easier for one to see the folly in others than in oneself. By pointing out the stupidity of making policy decisions based on SAT ranking, I hope teachers will internalize the error of making decisions about their students based on ranking classroom data. It is easier to criticize the politicians than it is to correct the same error in one's own world.

The most publicized ranking data are SAT comparisons. The explanations and graphs in this chapter argue that decisions based on SAT or any other ranking is folly. Tables 16-1 and 16-2 display ranked 1995 math and verbal SAT scores by state. A simple look at these scores would indicate that Iowa is wonderful and Connecticut is not so wonderful. When these data are added to the knowledge that Connecticut spends more money per student per year than Iowa, one begins to wonder if Connecticut's money is being wasted.

Figure 16-1 is a scatter diagram of 1995 math SAT scores. The scatter diagram shows a negative correlation between percentage of students taking the test and the state average score. The more students who take the test, the lower the scores. States that wish to have high SAT scores have figured out that the solution is simple: restrict access to the test.

Figure 16-2 displays the same information in a matrix. This matrix also shows a negative correlation between the percentage of students taking the test and the statewide average score, with some variation. Perfect correlation would have placed all of the states on the same diagonal. In math, the states are on nine diagonals of the

TABLE 16-1.   1995 mathematics SAT results by state.

State	Annual investment	Percentage	Math	Verbal
ND	$4636	5	592	515
IA	5442	5	583	516
MN	5795	9	579	506
WI	6987	9	572	501
SD	4918	5	563	505
UT	3626	4	563	513
IL	5262	13	560	488
KS	5893	9	557	503
NE	5302	9	556	494
MO	5002	9	550	495
MI	6783	11	549	484

TABLE 16-1—*Continued.*

State	Annual investment	Percentage	Math	Verbal
TN	$4535	12	543	497
MS	3697	4	540	498
AL	4458	8	538	491
MT	5619	21	536	473
OK	4323	9	536	491
LA	4934	9	535	486
NM	5411	11	530	485
WY	5939	10	525	476
AR	4106	6	523	482
KY	5611	11	522	477
CO	5500	29	518	462
OH	5911	23	515	460
ID	4227	15	511	468
OR	6229	51	499	448
AZ	4304	27	496	448
WA	5964	48	494	443
NH	6393	70	491	444
AK	9934	47	489	445
CA	4647	45	485	417
WV	6014	17	484	448
NV	5170	30	483	434
HI	6143	57	482	407
MD	6720	64	479	430
NJ	9889	70	478	420
CT	8604	81	477	431
MA	6940	80	477	430
TX	5492	47	474	419
NY	9300	74	473	419
VT	7165	68	472	429
FL	5683	48	469	420
ME	6366	68	469	427
DE	7146	68	468	429
VA	5664	65	468	428
IN	5618	58	467	415
RI	7348	70	463	425
PA	7567	70	461	419
NC	5065	60	454	411
GA	4976	65	448	406
DC	8682	53	445	412
SC	4726	58	443	401

TABLE 16-2. 1995 verbal SAT results by state.

State	Annual investment	Percentage	Math	Verbal
IA	$5442	5	583	516
ND	4636	5	592	515
UT	3626	4	563	513
MN	5795	9	579	506
SD	4918	5	563	505
KS	5893	9	557	503
WI	6987	9	572	501
MS	3697	4	540	498
TN	4535	12	543	497
MO	5002	9	550	495
NE	5302	9	556	494
AL	4458	8	538	491
OK	4323	9	536	491
IL	5262	13	560	488
LA	4934	9	535	486
NM	5411	11	530	485
MI	6783	11	549	484
AR	4106	6	523	482
KY	5611	11	522	477
WY	5939	10	525	476
MT	5619	21	536	473
ID	4227	15	511	468
CO	5500	29	518	462
OH	5911	23	515	460
OR	6229	51	499	448
AZ	4304	27	496	448
WV	6014	17	484	448
AK	9934	47	489	445
NH	6393	70	491	444
WA	5964	48	494	443
NV	5170	30	483	434
CT	8604	81	477	431
MD	6720	64	479	430
MA	6940	80	477	430
VT	7165	68	472	429
DE	7146	68	468	429
VA	5664	65	468	428
ME	6366	68	469	427
RI	7348	70	463	425
NJ	9889	70	478	420

TABLE 16-2—*Continued.*

State	Annual investment	Percentage	Math	Verbal
FL	$5683	48	469	420
TX	5492	47	474	419
NY	9300	74	473	419
PA	7567	70	461	419
CA	4647	45	485	417
IN	5618	58	467	415
DC	8682	53	445	412
NC	5065	60	454	411
HI	6143	57	482	407
GA	4976	65	448	406
SC	4726	58	443	401

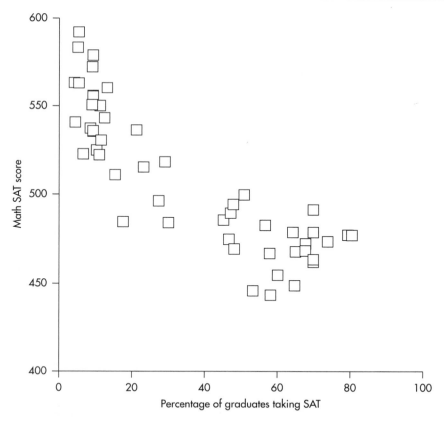

FIGURE 16-1.   1995 mathematics SAT scatter diagram.

	2–10%	11–18%	19–26%	27–34%	35–42%
578–592	Iowa Minnesota North Dakota	2	1		
563–577	South Dakota Wisconsin Utah	3	2	1	
548–562	Nebraska Kansas Missouri	Illinois Michigan	3	2	1
533–547	Oklahoma Alabama Louisiana Mississippi	Tennessee	Montana	3	2
518–532	Arkansas Wyoming	Kentucky New Mexico	5	Colorado	3
503–517	8	Idaho	Ohio	5	4
488–502	9	8	7	Arizona	5
473–487		West Virginia	8	Nevada	6
458–472			9	8	7
443–457				9	8

FIGURE 16-2. 1995 mathematics SAT matrix.

	43–50%	51–58%	59–66%	67–74%	75–82%
578–592					
563–577					
548–562					
533–547	1				
518–532	2	1			
503–517	3	2	1		
488–502	Alaska Washington	Oregon	2	New Hampshire	
473–487	Texas California	Hawaii	Maryland	New Jersey New York	Connecticut Massachusetts
458–472	Florida	Indiana	Virginia	Delaware Maine Pennsylvania Rhode Island Vermont	2
443–457	7	Washington, D.C. South Carolina	Georgia North Carolina	4	3

FIGURE 16-2. *Continued.*

19 possible, showing that some factors other than percentage taking the test are at work. The histogram showing the range of states on diagonals is Figure 16-3. The states can now be studied according to their diagonal number. The thinking behind this ranking is that being in the upper-right-hand cell of the 100-cell matrix is ideal. This would mean almost all high school graduates were administered the SAT and the scores ranked among the highest states. No state achieved this position on the matrix. The first diagonal with states was labeled diagonal 1, the second diagonal with states was labeled 2, and so on, until all nine diagonals with states were labeled.

Now a different view of states and SAT scores is available. New Hampshire, Connecticut, and Massachusetts share diagonal 1. Diagonal 2 includes New Jersey and New York, while diagonal 6 includes Washington, D.C., and 10 other states.

I am not advocating the continued use of athletic-type ranking statistics in education, but if America insists on it, then it should follow all the athletic rules. Teams that play only 10 percent of the games in a season are not included in that season's ranking. This ranking, which puts the three Eastern states on top, may also be flawed, but it is far superior to a system that allows a state to test 5 percent of its high school graduates and be touted as number one.

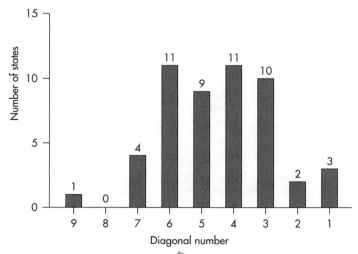

FIGURE 16-3. Histogram of states on diagonals—Mathematics.

If America persists in using ranking as a decision-making tool, then policy makers should at least ensure that all states complete the season. With 15 states having played 10 percent or less of the games, they should forfeit the season.

Without the matrix it is easy for education's critics to use only ranked data and jump to the false conclusion that, since Utah is ranked higher than Massachusetts, for example, money has nothing to do with quality of education. Figure 16-4 shows the SAT verbal scatter diagram, and Figure 16-5 shows the SAT matrix for the verbal scores. The states are more alike on the verbal test, having been plotted on only eight of the 19 diagonals without any empty diagonals. Figure 16-6 shows the number of states on each verbal diagonal.

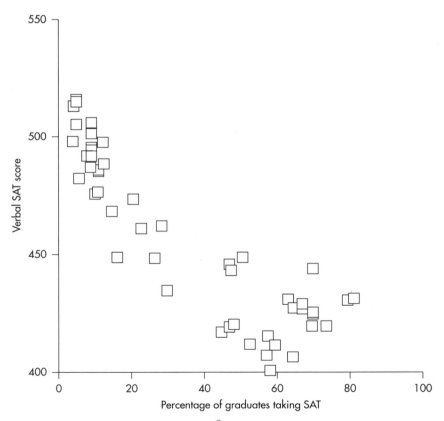

FIGURE 16-4. 1995 verbal SAT scatter diagram.

509–520	Iowa Utah North Dakota 2	1			
497–508	Minnesota Kansas South Dakota Wisconsin Mississippi	Tennessee 2	1		
485–496	Missouri Nebraska Louisiana Alabama Oklahoma	Illinois New Mexico 3	2	1	
473–484	Arkansas Wyoming	Kentucky Michigan	Montana	3	2
461–472	7	Idaho	5	Colorado	3
449–460	8	7	Arizona	5	4
437–448		West Virginia	7	Ohio	5
425–436			8	Nevada	6
413–424				8	7
401–412					8
	3–10%	11–18%	19–26%	27–34%	35–42%

FIGURE 16-5. 1995 verbal SAT matrix.

43–50%	51–58%	59–66%	67–74%	75–82%	
					509–520
					497–508
					485–496
1					473–484
2	1				461–472
3	2	1			449–460
Alaska Washington	Oregon	2	New Hampshire		437–448
5	4	Virginia Maryland	Delaware Maine Rhode Island Vermont	Connecticut Massachusetts	425–436
Florida Texas California	Indiana	4	Pennsylvania New York New Jersey	2	413–424
7	Hawaii South Carolina Washington, D.C.	Georgia North Carolina	4	3	401–412

FIGURE 16-5. *Continued.*

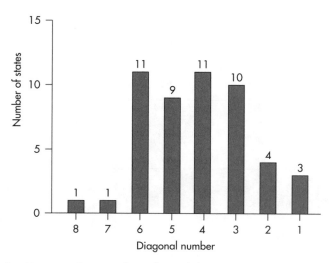

FIGURE 16-6. Histogram of states on diagonals—Verbal.

A second related set of matrices is now possible. On the vertical axes are the diagonal numbers from the verbal and mathematics matrices, and on the horizontal axes are the average dollar investments per student per year.[2] Figures 16-7 and 16-8 allow a comparison of the diagonal ranking with the investment per student. Are states with a higher per-pupil investment on the higher-numbered diagonals? Yes, this is generally true with a few exceptions. Connecticut, New York, and New Jersey invest heavily in the education of their youth and the results show. Mississippi, Arkansas, and Idaho, on the other hand, invest less and the results are less acceptable. Utah and North Dakota are getting a good return on their investment, whereas Alaska taxpayers aren't receiving, according to SAT results, what one would expect. There is a positive correlation between investment per student and diagonal ranking. Now data are available for decision making, instead of the political falsehood that money makes no difference.

The matrix look at the SAT scores was not developed to be the most comprehensive SAT analysis available, but to demonstrate the fallacy of decision making from ranking data. To move from change to continual improvement, educators and their leaders must drop ranking as a decision-making tool.

No ranking comparison documents improvement. A school district can improve its ranking because neighboring districts scored worse, because of good luck, or because of actual improvement. Nobody knows. (Good luck seems like a nonsense reason for higher scores, yet every teacher knows that some year's classes are better than others. Some years a school district will have an exceptional group of third graders. The scores will rise because of good luck. Next year's scores will return to normal. This is bad luck.)

Test scores also improve because school districts move outstanding teachers into the grade level the state has chosen for statewide assessment. The overall quality of graduates from the district hasn't improved because students still spend a year with poor-quality teachers, but the scores go up. California changed its assessment of reading and mathematics from grade three to grade four. Slowly but surely, personnel adjustments will be made across the state.

In the early 1960s General Motors was losing money in four divisions and making money in one. Overall the corporation was losing money. The head of the one division, Chevrolet, designed cars to compete with Cadillac, Pontiac, Oldsmobile, and Buick. His bonus was superb, Chevrolet became number one, but the corporation lost as a whole. Dr. Deming calls this suboptimization. The whole is not optimized; only a section is gaining.

The current American education system mirrors the experience of General Motors. Twenty percent of the students, schools, and school districts are ranked high; the others are ranked as losers. If Americans intend to be competitive in the global economy, everyone must determine that improvement is more important than ranking.

	$3626–4256	$4257–4887	$4888–5518	$5519–6149	$6150–6780
1					New Hampshire
2					
3		North Dakota		Minnesota	Maryland Maine Oregon
4	Utah		Colorado Illinois South Dakota	Hawaii Washington Virginia Montana	
5		California Tennessee	Texas Nebraska Missouri Georgia	Kansas Indiana	
6	Mississippi	South Carolina Alabama Oklahoma	Louisiana New Mexico	Ohio Florida Kentucky	
7	Arkansas	Idaho	Nevada	Wyoming	
8			North Carolina		
9				West Virginia	

Diagonal numbers from 1995 correlation of math SAT and percentage taking SAT

Investment per pupil per year

FIGURE 16-7.   SAT mathematics and investment per pupil matrix.

$6781–7411	$7412–8042	$8674–9304	$9305–9935	$9750–10,499	
Massachusetts		Connecticut			1
			New York	New Jersey	2
Rhode Island Vermont Delaware	Pennsylvania				3
Wisconsin Michigan				Alaska	4
					5
			Washington, D.C.		6
					7
					8
					9

FIGURE 16-7. *Continued.*

Diagonal numbers from 1995 correlation of verbal SAT and percentage taking SAT

	$3626–4256	$4257–4887	$4888–5518	$5519–6149	$6150–6780
1					New Hampshire
2					Maine
3	Utah	Tennessee North Dakota	Iowa	Virginia	Oregon Maryland
4	Mississippi		South Dakota New Mexico Illinois	Colorado Washington Indiana Kansas Minnesota	
5		Alabama Oklahoma	Kentucky Georgia North Carolina Nebraska Louisiana Missouri	Montana	
6	Idaho Arkansas	Arizona South Carolina California		Texas Hawaii Florida Wyoming Ohio	
7			Nevada		
8				West Virginia	

Investment per pupil per year

FIGURE 16-8. SAT verbal and investment per pupil matrix.

$6781–7411	$7412–8042	$8674–9304	$9305–9935	$9750–10,499	
Massachusetts		Connecticut			1
Rhode Island Vermont Delaware					2
	Pennsylvania		New York	New Jersey	3
Wisconsin				Alaska	4
Michigan					5
			Washington, D.C.		6
					7
					8

FIGURE 16-8. *Continued.*

Notes

1. W. Edwards Deming, *Schools and Communities Cooperating for Quality—Lessons for Leaders* (seminar sponsored by American Association of School Administrators, Alexandria, Va., 1990 handout), ch. 2, p. 4.
2. *1995 Vital Statistics,* Washington, D.C.: National School Boards Association, pp. A26–A31.

Chapter 17
PRIORITY MATRIX

The priority matrix is a tool designed to help leaders better listen to their customers. Figure 17-1 is a blank priority matrix designed for learning the relative importance of up to eight items. The priority matrix can be made for any number of items, but this sample shows eight. After the items are brainstormed, they are placed in any order on the blank priority matrix. Participants then compare each item to the others. If item 1 is more important than item 2, then a 1 is circled. Next, item 1 is contrasted with item 3, item 4, item 5, and so on. Each of the eight items is contrasted to the other seven items.

Name: _____   Topic: _____

Option	Item	Voting matrix								Totals	
1		1 2	1 3	1 4	1 5	1 6	1 7	1 8		1	
2		2 3	2 4	2 5	2 6	2 7	2 8			2	
3		3 4	3 5	3 6	3 7	3 8				3	
4		4 5	4 6	4 7	4 8					4	
5		5 6	5 7	5 8						5	
6		6 7	6 8							6	
7		7 8								7	
8										8	
										Total	28

FIGURE 17-1.   Blank priority matrix.

After a chapter on the ills of ranking, it seems contradictory to include the priority matrix, which ranks concepts and opinions. It is not harmful, however, to rank opinions during the decision-making process. It is the ranking of people and their achievements that is harmful to the improvement process.

After all of the rows are completed, the number of times each item was selected is tabulated and recorded at the far right. The totals from each participant are then added up for a grand total; if the sum is not 28, an error in counting or addition has been made. The results communicate the most important to least important on a topic for which opinion, rather than results, is needed.

The priority matrix is a superb tool in helping educators make complex decisions, such as what can be done to slow the loss of enthusiasm for learning or ways to improve learning. It is helpful for a teacher to rank from high to low the relative importance of students' ideas, but ranking the students themselves is harmful. For example, seventh graders, in Figure 17-5, said that homework was the number one reason why students lose enthusiasm for learning. This is a ranking that teachers should listen to and explore in depth. Good can come from ranking opinions, whereas no good can come from ranking people. Examples of opinion ranking are provided in the figures that follow.

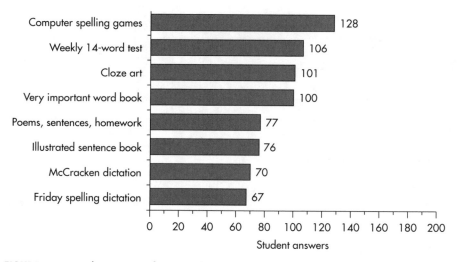

FIGURE 17-2. What were your favorite spelling activities?

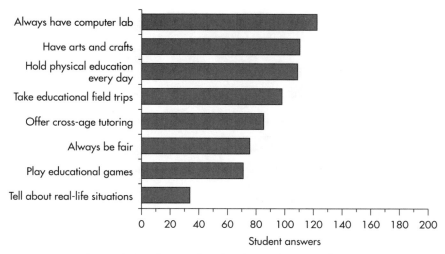

FIGURE 17-3. What are the best things teachers do to keep students excited about school?

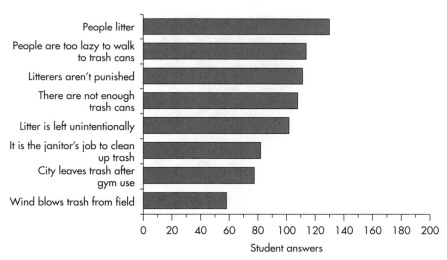

FIGURE 17-4. Why is there trash on campus?

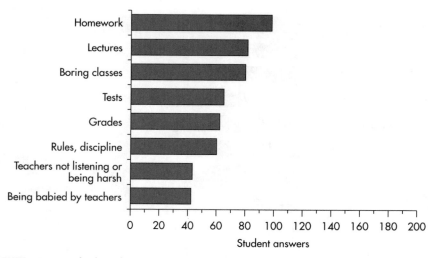

FIGURE 17-5. Why do students lose their enthusiasm for learning?

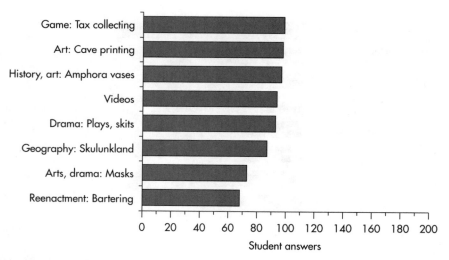

FIGURE 17-6. What are your favorite social studies activities?

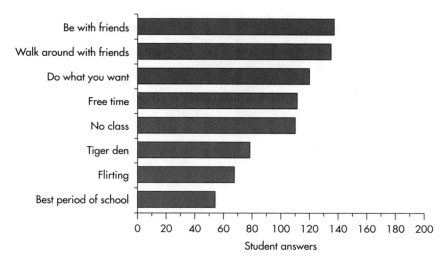

FIGURE 17-7.   What are the best things about lunch hour?

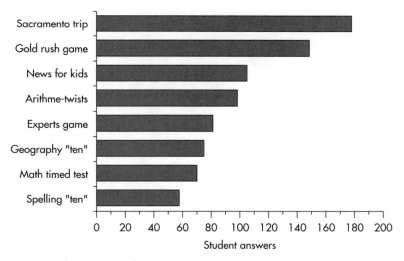

FIGURE 17-8.   What are the best learning activities?

Chapter 18
CAUSE-AND-EFFECT (FISHBONE) DIAGRAM

The major advantages of the cause-and-effect, or fishbone, diagram are (1) it helps people direct their energies toward a common aim, and (2) it forces people to study the many facets that influence an event. First a group must determine what to place in the blank rectangle at the right end of the fishbone; this is the effect. Sometimes this determination is easy. The question "Why are students losing enthusiasm for learning?" is easy to ask. On other occasions the contents of the rectangle—the effect—might be the aim for the whole enterprise. Such a deliberation could take considerable time, debate, and consensus.

Several years ago I picked up a $1.00 pamphlet on advice for leaders. The most interesting piece of advice was, "Give only one reason for a decision." The logic behind this advice was if a leader provides all of the reasons for a decision more people will be able to find a reason with which they disagree, and they will fight the decision with more ammunition. The author of the advice was correct in one sense; most people do believe decisions are made for only one reason. Even if they disagree with the rationale given by the boss, they do not say, "I think the boss made the decision for these five reasons." Most likely, they substitute the boss' stated reason with another, single motivation they believe to be at work.

In an environment of quality and teamwork the cause-and-effect diagram quickly demonstrates that many causes influence any particular effect. Almost always there is more than one reason or cause for a decision.

Once the effect to be studied is determined and written in the rectangle, the group's next job is to determine whether the five generic *bones* of the diagram (equipment, people, material, methods, environment) are adequate for studying the effect. If not, they must add or delete bones. When all aspects, or causes, of the problem are identified with the appropriate bones, the process continues with identifying *sub-bones*.

Cause-and-effect diagrams have two directions: positive and negative. When studying a positive effect, one could ask, "How do we assure mathematical competence in our high school graduates?" Parents, students, staff, and community would all use the same tool to write sub-bones. Teamwork develops because everyone sees their contribution toward meeting the aim of mathematical competence in graduates. Figure 18-1 shows an example of such a fishbone written by high school students.

The second use of the cause-and-effect diagram is to research why a negative is occurring. For example, a group might study, "Why does our school district have a 90 percent dropout rate in mathematics?" (To calculate the dropout rate, divide the number of students in senior-level math by the number of first graders. Subtract the answer from 100. For example, a school district with 500 first graders but only 50 seniors in calculus has a 90 percent dropout rate.) Figure 18-2, also written by students, describes reasons why they drop out of mathematics.

The cause-and-effect diagram is useful for most purposes. Figure 18-3 is a diagram written by seventh graders studying the question of enthusiasm loss. The diagram shows from the students' perspective why they lose their enthusiasm for learning. Unlike the priority matrix, the cause-and-effect diagram does not rank the reasons.

Dr. Deming showed audiences the opposite of the cause-and-effect diagram. He called it, "Everybody doing their best,"[1] a simple diagram of 20 arrows pointing in different directions. "Will best efforts bring improvement?" he would ask. "Unfortunately, no: Best efforts are not sufficient. Best efforts must be guided by knowledge."[2] Figure 18-4 is a reproduction of Dr. Deming's diagram.

I have used the cause-and-effect diagram for help in decision making in all aspects of school administration. Some issues have been related to instruction, some to personnel, and some to the business office. The tool works equally well in all areas. Because this book is focused on improved learning and maintaining enthusiasm for learning, I have chosen to include only fishbones that demonstrate the tool's usefulness in studying these two aspects of schooling. I would not want readers to conclude, however, that the

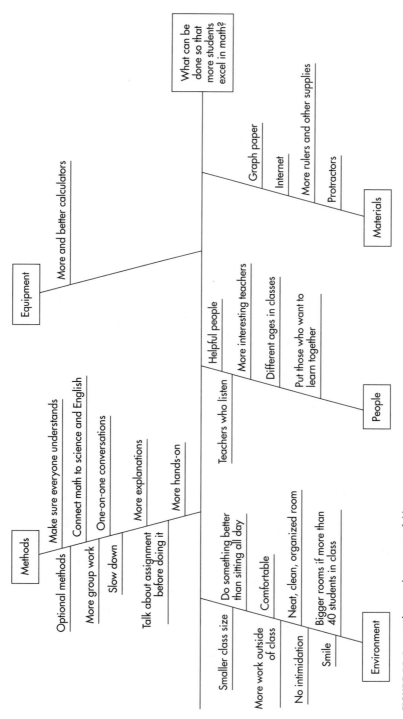

FIGURE 18-1. Mathematical competence fishbone.

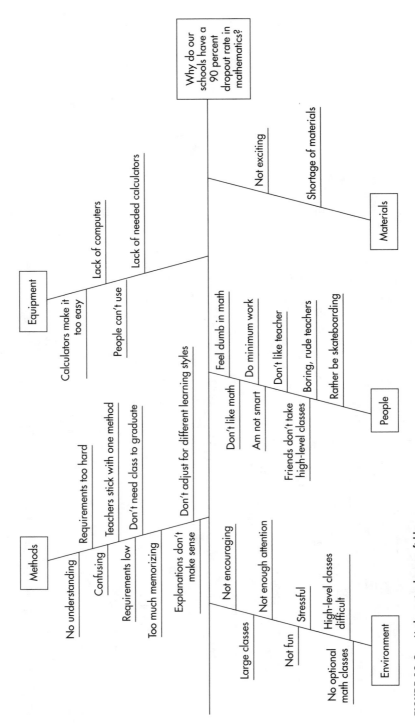

FIGURE 18-2. Mathematics dropouts fishbone.

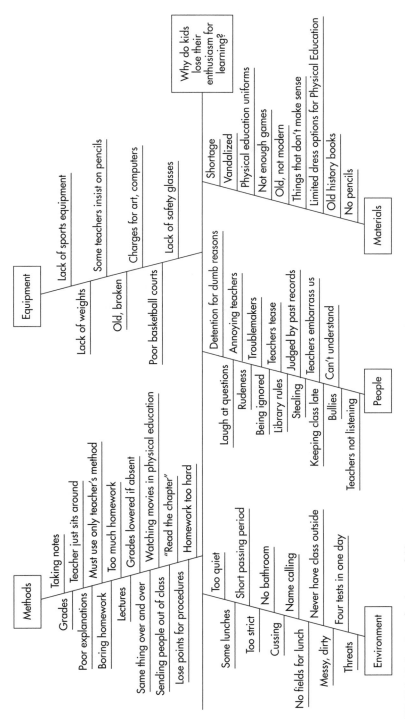

FIGURE 18-3. Loss of enthusiasm fishbone.

163

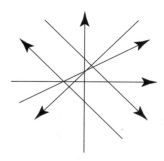
Everybody doing their best

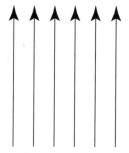
What citizens want

FIGURE 18-4. Everybody doing their best.

fishbone diagram is limited to instructional issues. Teachers could easily involve students in preparing a fishbone regarding behavior on the playground or parents coming to open house.

In summary, the fishbone is a listening and consensus-building tool to help groups reach agreements (1) that they expect to cause improvements, and (2) regarding what is causing a desired or undesirable effect. Whether studying a current state or future state, the cause-and-effect diagram provides a comprehensive view of organizational influences. It provides structured, purposeful brainstorming rather than a list of conflicting ideas.

Notes

1. W. Edwards Deming, American Association of School Administrators Conference, Washington, D.C., January 1992.
2. Ibid.

Chapter 19
SCATTER DIAGRAM

The scatter diagram belongs in the lunchroom, for it seems it isn't very long into a sandwich (somewhere between the second and third bite) when a complaint is voiced. About two chews later somebody else claims to know the cause or has the solution to the complaint. More than likely this person has an opinion with no data.

The scatter diagram is the quality tool to provide data for the lunchroom discussion. To illustrate the scatter diagram, I will share an opinion for which I have no data: Less data correlates with louder voices and more data correlates with quieter voices.

A scatter diagram is set up with two variables. In this example the variables are the volume of voice used by the person with the answer to the complaint and the amount of data to back up the answer. To complete this scatter diagram one would place a dot for each lunchroom conversation. After 30 to 50 dots were placed, there would be sufficient data to know if the hypothesis were correct (that is, the louder the voice the less the data).

Five possible patterns appear on scatter diagrams.[1] The first pattern would support my hypothesis; it would show a strong negative correlation between voice and data. In other words, the less the data, the louder the voice.

The scatter diagram in Figure 19-1 would support my hypothesis that an increase in volume correlates with a lack of data. As the data increases there is a strong probability that the volume is reduced.

The second pattern (see Figure 19-2) shows a possible negative correlation. More data might decrease voice volume, but there are other factors at work other than the amount of data. Figures 16-1 and 16-4, which correlate SAT scores with the percentage of graduates tested, demonstrate this second pattern. There is a correlation, but other factors are at work. Figures 16-7 and 16-8, which show investment per pupil, would indicate that finances are a possible factor.

Scatter diagram correlating voice volume and data available

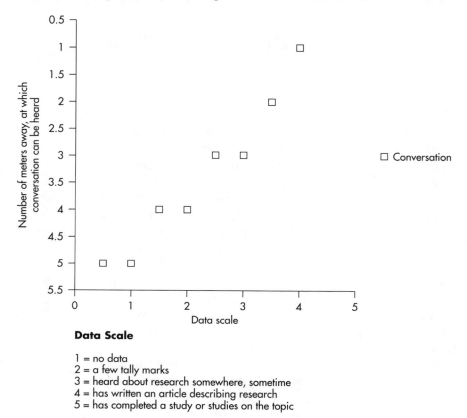

Data Scale

1 = no data
2 = a few tally marks
3 = heard about research somewhere, sometime
4 = has written an article describing research
5 = has completed a study or studies on the topic

FIGURE 19-1. Scatter diagram with strong negative correlation.

Scatter diagram correlating voice volume and data available

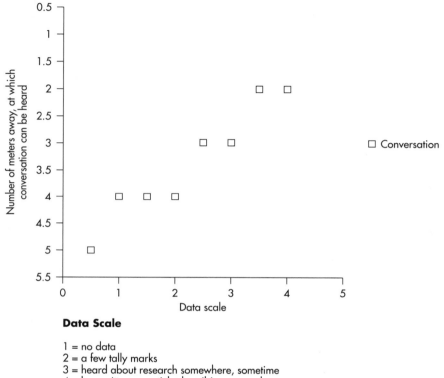

Data Scale

1 = no data
2 = a few tally marks
3 = heard about research somewhere, sometime
4 = has written an article describing research
5 = has completed a study or studies on the topic

FIGURE 19-2. Scatter diagram with possible negative correlation.

The third scatter diagram pattern (see Figure 19-3) shows that the amount of data has nothing to do with voice volume; variable voice is not dependent on variable data. This pattern would indicate that my hypothesis is wrong.

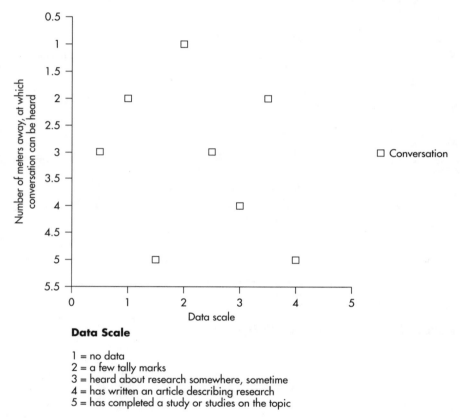

FIGURE 19-3. Scatter diagram showing no correlation.

Figure 19-4 shows a pattern that indicates the opposite of my hypothesis is possibly true. It indicates that more data tend to increase voice volume in lunchroom debates.

Scatter diagram correlating voice volume and data available

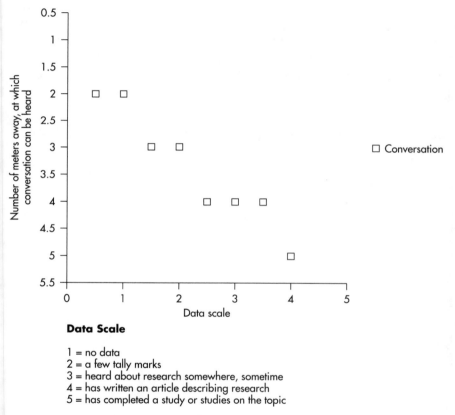

Data Scale

1 = no data
2 = a few tally marks
3 = heard about research somewhere, sometime
4 = has written an article describing research
5 = has completed a study or studies on the topic

FIGURE 19-4. Scatter diagram with possible positive correlation.

The last scatter diagram pattern, shown in Figure 19-5, indicates that the opposite of my hypothesis is true: An increase in data may increase voice volume. The correlation is strong.

The following figures are examples of actual educational scatter diagrams. Figures 19-6 and 19-7 provide data on the continuing debate about standardized multiple-choice tests. Figure 19-6 compares reading scores and students' reading levels as measured on a continuum (the continuum is shown in Table 19-1). The data indicate that the two variables are somewhat positively correlated in that a high Comprehensive Test of Basic Skills (CTBS) score generally means a high reading ability as measured by the teacher. Figure 19-7 compares district third graders' CTBS scores with scores

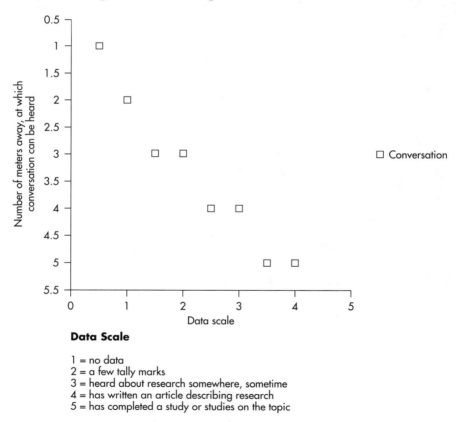

Scatter diagram correlating voice volume and data available

Data Scale

1 = no data
2 = a few tally marks
3 = heard about research somewhere, sometime
4 = has written an article describing research
5 = has completed a study or studies on the topic

FIGURE 19-5. Scatter diagram showing strong positive correlation.

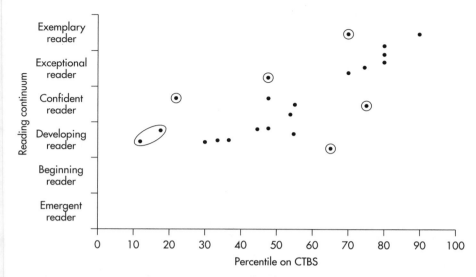

FIGURE 19-6. Scatter diagram comparing reading as measured by standardized test with reading continuum.

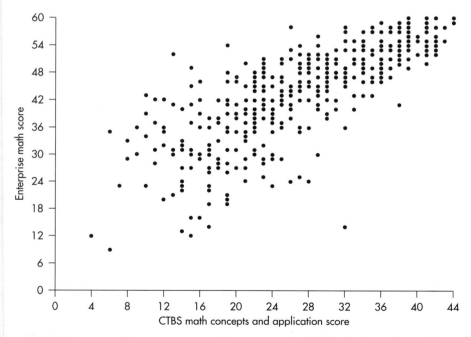

FIGURE 19-7. Scatter diagram comparing mathematics as measured by standardized test and district-written exam.

TABLE 19-1. Reading continuum.

Grades K–2

Emergent reader	*Beginning reader*	*Development reader*
• Enjoys being read to	• Focuses on print	• Developing a
• Relies on memory for	• Locates a given word	confidence
reading	in a known sentence	• Becomes an efficient
• Joins in the oral	• Begins to use word	silent reader
reading of familiar	identification	(sometimes whispers
stories, especially	strategies	when reading difficult
those with a rhythmic	• Shows some	text)
language	awareness of title,	• Develops further
• Shows curiosity about	author, and illustrator	understanding of
print	• Reads known and	punctuation (question
• Understands about	predictable and other	marks, quotation
print; directionality,	beginning books	marks)
format of a book,	• Understands sound	• Increases and refines
sentences, word, line,	and symbol	use of word
letter, spaces,	relationships	identification
beginning and end		strategies to gain
• Tells a story from		meaning
pictures		• Shows familiarity with
• Answers questions		titles, authors, and
about a teacher-read		illustrators
story		• Selects book for
• Chooses to look at		reading
books as a free-time		independently
activity		• Reads with an
		appropriate level of
		skill and
		understanding both
		familiar and
		unfamiliar text

on a district test of math standards. Most teachers believe the district test is more accurate; the CTBS test states that more students are less competent in math. In the teachers' opinions, these students cannot meet the standardized requirement to compute quickly.

These data support the typical test publisher claim that multiple-choice tests are accurate for groups. Figure 19-6 also indicates that for seven students (the points circled on the scatter diagram) the two indicators of reading ability don't correlate.

Grades 3–5

Confident reader
- Self-motivated, pursues own interests through reading
- Capable of reading in all subject areas
- With direction, locates and draws on a variety of sources to research a topic
- Reads to others with appropriate expression
- Automatically applies multiple strategies to figure out words

Exceptional reader
- An enthusiastic and reflective reader
- Reads a wide range and variety of texts, including advanced materials
- Uses many appropriate strategies to understand the reading selections
- Self-selects challenging books

Exemplary reader
- Thinks divergently, takes risks, makes predictions, expresses ideas
- Explores multiple possibilities of meaning
- Fills in gaps, uses clues and evidence to draw conclusions
- Can recognize and deal with ambiguities in text disagreeing or questioning
- Can demonstrate understanding of the work as a whole
- Can show aesthetic appreciation of the text
- Makes connections between the text(s) and own ideas and experiences
- Can retell, summarize, and/or paraphrase with purpose

These seven exceptions support educators' belief that standardized, multiple-choice tests are not accurate for individuals. At least, the results from one day of testing on a standardized, multiple-choice test don't match 180 days of teacher observation.

From the same third grade class is another scatter diagram, Figure 19-8, contrasting reading speed with placement on the reading continuum. In this instance only two students (circled) are outside the band of strong positive correlation. Reading speed

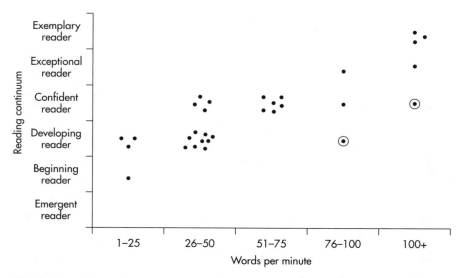

FIGURE 19-8. Scatter diagram comparing reading as measured by reading continuum with reading speed.

for this study was measured by having the students read grade-appropriate material for one minute. Words not known by the student were provided by the timer, but not counted in the final words-per-minute tabulation.

Figure 19-9 displays a possible positive correlation between fourth graders' knowledge of math concepts and their ability to solve open-ended math problems scored on a 1-to-6 rubric. Nine students' ability to solve problems (knowledge) was not strongly correlated to math concepts (information). Using the criteria from earlier in this chapter, math concepts and problem-solving (knowledge) have a possible positive correlation. As math concept increases, problem-solving knowledge may also increase, but there are more factors influencing problem-solving success than concept attainment.

Scatter diagrams don't prove cause and effect, but they do display relationships that are helpful in decision making. The fourth grade National Assessment of Educational Progress (NAEP) is a case in point. Scatter diagrams can be prepared for various hypotheses regarding cause for high or low performance. For example, is there a correlation between NAEP score and teacher

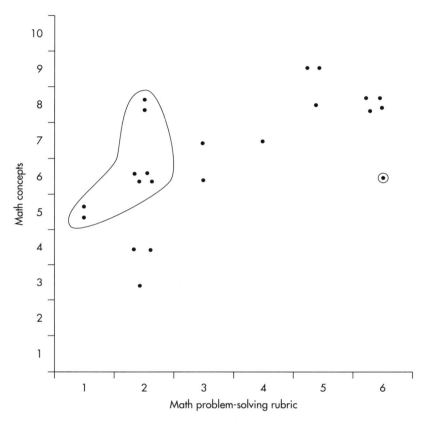

FIGURE 19-9. Scatter diagram comparing mathematics concepts with mathematics problem solving.

salary? NAEP and class size? NAEP and kindergarten entry age? NAEP and winter temperature? Perhaps students in cold states read more, and thus better, than those in warm states. Figures 19-10 through 19-13 show scatter diagrams correlating NAEP results and these four hypotheses.

The scatter diagram is an excellent decision-making tool for ruling out causes. For example, the four NAEP scatter diagrams don't conclusively document a single cause for California's NAEP score, but they do rule out teacher salary and kindergarten entry age as causes.

One observation people make on seeing Figure 14-9, Enthusiasm by subject for eighth grade, is that it looks like hands-on

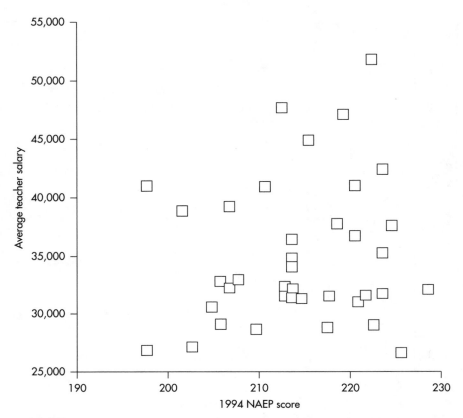

FIGURE 19-10. Scatter diagram comparing NAEP fourth grade reading with teacher salaries.

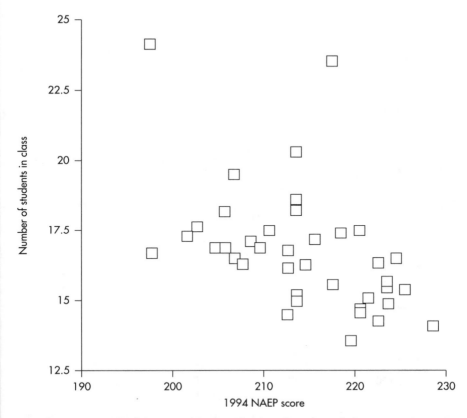

FIGURE 19-11. Scatter diagram comparing NAEP fourth grade reading with class size.

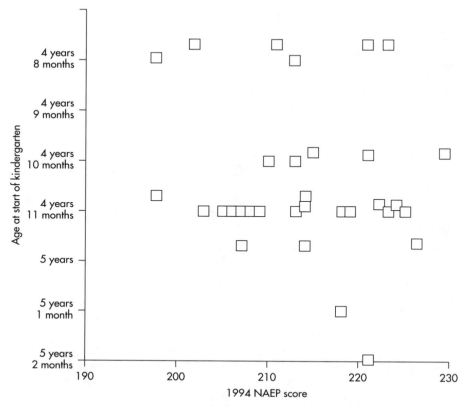

FIGURE 19-12. Scatter diagram comparing NAEP fourth grade reading with kindergarten entry age.

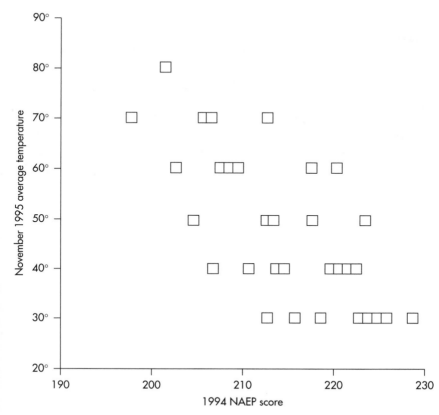

FIGURE 19-13.   Scatter diagram comparing NAEP fourth grade reading with winter temperatures.

subjects help students better maintain their enthusiasm for learning than other subjects. Twenty teachers were asked to state what percentage of school assignments involved hands-on activities. They reflected on their view of education as a whole, not their particular classroom. Next, the average number of happy faces students gave for each school subject on an attitude survey was correlated with the percentage of hands-on activities. Figure 19-14 shows the resultant scatter diagram. It documents a positive correlation between time spent on hands-on activities and students' responses to the attitude survey. The higher the percentage of hands-on activities, the higher the percentage of happy faces.

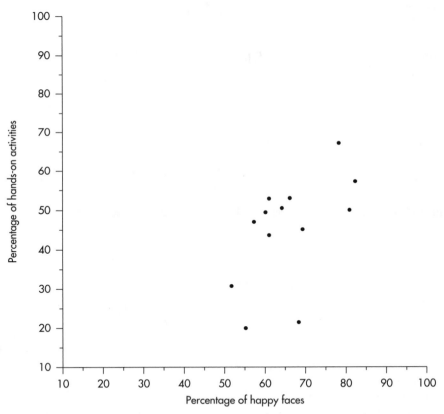

FIGURE 19-14. Scatter diagram comparing student attitudes with percentage of hands-on activities.

Most school districts can easily document the number of students who have moved during a particular school year. Often school employees want to have some influence on the transience of their pupils. The scatter diagram can provide some insights into reasons for student transience. Perhaps economic factors are so strong that educators cannot affect this; perhaps they can. The scatter diagram in Figure 19-15 doesn't answer this question, but it does give insight into student enthusiasm as a factor. A possible correlation exists between percentage of happy faces and transiency rate. The schools with a high rate of student enthusiasm, seem to have less transience.

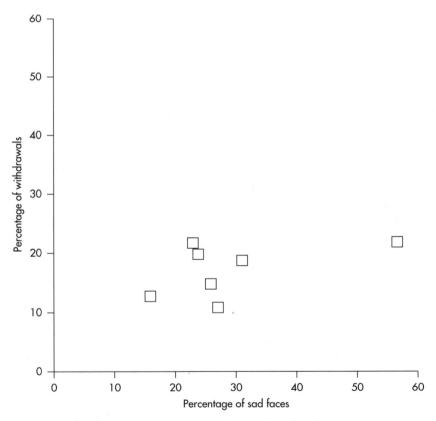

FIGURE 19-15. Scatter diagram comparing student attitudes with student transience.

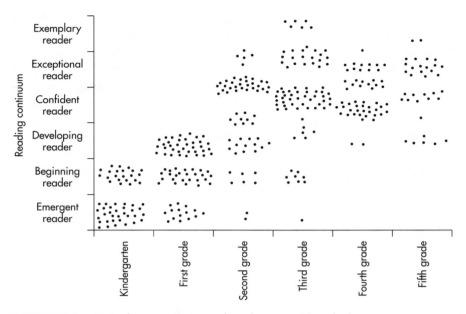

FIGURE 19-16. Scatter diagram comparing reading achievement with grade placement.

Most of the examples of scatter diagrams in this chapter are of classrooms. Scatter diagrams for a whole school, however, can be a powerful tool for a principal. The scatter diagram in Figure 19-16 shows a dot for every pupil in a K–5 school. The data were taken from report cards at midyear. So much of educational data masks over individual children, but the scatter diagram may prove to be the most powerful of the decision-making quality tools because every dot represents a child.

Two variations of scatter diagrams have been presented, one showing a negative correlation and the other a positive correlation. In a diagram showing positive correlation, both values increase at the same time. For example, an increase in funding shown in Figures 16-7 and 16-8 correlates with an increase in diagonal ranking. In a diagram showing negative correlation, the values relate, but in opposite directions. In Figures 16-1 and 16-2, as the percentage of test takers increases, the average SAT score decreases.

Most people reading this book have probably studied correlation coefficients. But how often is this statistical tool used in the daily life of teachers and administrators? The answer is somewhere between rarely and never. The scatter diagram, by contrast, is simple to use and gives much data for decision making.

Note

1. *The Memory Jogger for Education* (Methuen, Mass: Goal/QPC, 1992), p. 44.

Chapter 20
CONTROL CHART

One of the most important tools for helping educators escape the perils of blaming and ranking is the control chart. "Nothing is more important in education than differences between common cause and special cause."[1] Dr. Deming credits Dr. Walter Shewhart with formulating the two basic uses of control charts.[2]

The first use of the control chart is for making judgments. Do the data show any special-cause variation? If not, the variation is all common cause, meaning the variation is built into the system. Common-cause variation, because it is built into the system, will continue unchanged unless improvement efforts are successful.

The shifting of sands in desert areas can illustrate what Drs. Shewhart and Deming meant by common- and special-cause variation. In Albuquerque, New Mexico, where I spent eight delightful childhood years, it seemed the sand moved daily. The amount of shifting sand varied from day to day. The only thing for certain on any given day was that less sand or more sand would shift the next day. This is common-cause variation. Once in a while, however, the local rain combined with the moisture off the Sandia Mountains to fill the arroyos. Whatever sand was in the way of this water was displaced. This is an example of special-cause variation. A bored journalist could rank sand storms, but the worst day of blowing sand isn't special-cause variation. It just happens to be the day the most sand moves within a system that blows sand on many days.

The second use of control charts is for studying ongoing operations. The purpose is to determine whether an operation for which constancy is desirable has any special-cause variation. An example is the school district financial reserve. The ending balance plus the ongoing reserve will vary from year to year. A special-cause dip in reserves, however, can wreak havoc on an entire organization. On the other hand, a special-cause of extra reserves is a positive event.

I have found that using control charts for judgment is the most valuable. School leaders are continually faced with data showing variation among classrooms, schools, school districts, and states. One must heed Dr. Deming's admonition that managers should know which of the workers (students, classrooms, school, districts, states) are above and which are below the control limits of the system. Dr. Deming quoted Dr. Joseph M. Juran, stating that the hard work begins once the special-cause variation is removed and "the important problems of improvement commence."[3] Managers need to know which elements are above and below the limits of their system, but once this is addressed, the difficult work of improvement starts.

Figures 20-1 and 20-2 display reading results from 15 different first grade classrooms at the end of two school years. The graphs, without the control limits, merely display the number of first graders who missed more than 70 words on a 100-word story in May. The cutoff of 70 errors was used for placement in Title I for second grade. Without the upper control limit and lower control limit, a leader has no way of ascertaining which classrooms, if any, are above or below the system. The typical assumption is that the classroom with the most Title I students is a problem. This, however, is decision making by ranking.

Once the control limits are placed on the graphs it can be seen that in 1992 two classrooms were special causes of variation and in 1993 there were no special-cause classrooms. One hundred percent of the variation in 1993 was a result of the system of instruction within the school district. In 1992, 93 percent of the variation was caused by the system (common cause) and 7 percent of the variation was special cause. Even though there is reason to be concerned about the two special-cause classrooms, the biggest issue, by far, is the common-cause variation. (One classroom had two students above the upper control limit and the other had four students above. These six students are 7 percent of the 84 total students identified for Title I.)

There are different types of control charts, each of which comes from different statistical rules. The p and c charts in this chapter are only two types. For a complete overview of control charts see *Improvement Tools for Education (K–12).*[4]

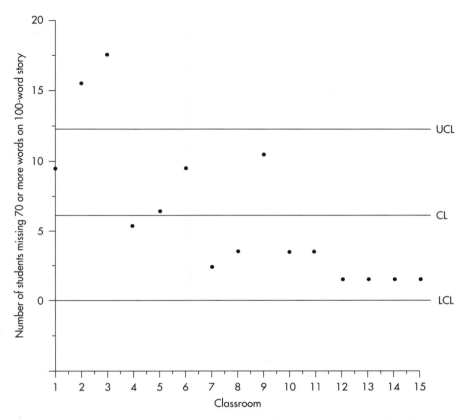

Variation in class 1 and classes 4 through 15 is due to common causes within the district's system. Variation in classes 2 and 3 is special; it is caused by factors not common to the rest of the district's system.

Central line = 6.33
UCL = 13.88
LCL = 0

FIGURE 20-1. First grade reading control chart showing special-cause variation.

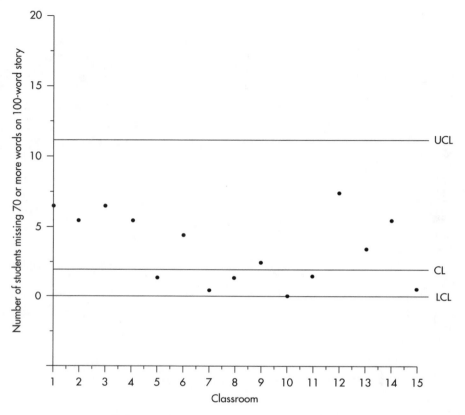

Variation in all classes is due to common causes within the district's system. There is no special-cause variation.

Central line = 4.06
UCL = 10.11
LCL = 0

FIGURE 20-2. First grade reading control chart showing common-cause variation.

The first control chart used for judgment at the end of the school year was a *c* (count) control chart. The formula for the *c* chart is as follows:[5]

$$\text{Upper control limit (UCL)} = x + \left(3\sqrt{x}\right)$$
$$\text{Lower control limit (LCL)} = x - \left(3\sqrt{x}\right)$$
$$\text{Central line} = \text{mean } (x)$$

The UCL describes the upper limit of common-cause variation. A particular state, district, school, classroom, or student above the UCL is a special case. Likewise, the LCL describes the lower limit of common-cause variation. Any entity below the LCL is special. Because the mean is displayed as a line it is called the central line. Average, mean, and central line are synonymous.

The following formula was applied to the data used in building Figure 20-1. The average number of students per class missing 70 or more words on a 100-word story was 6.33.

$$UCL = 6.33 + \left(3\sqrt{6.33}\right)$$
$$UCL = 13.87 \text{ or } 14$$

$$LCL = 6.33 - \left(3\sqrt{6.33}\right)$$
$$LCL = 6.33 - 7.54$$
$$LCL = 0$$

Susan Leddick, who worked extensively with Dr. Deming and helped write *Improvement Tools for Educators (K–12),* makes the following points about a *c* chart.

- It uses the raw count as the data to be plotted. In Figures 20-1 and 20-2 the actual number of children was counted.
- Each item being plotted can have multiple occurrences; there is no denominator. Often the reason a *c* chart must be chosen is that there is no possibility of ever having a denominator, as in the number of discipline problems in a school, since each student can commit an infraction more than once.

Dr. Deming stressed through his stories of workers that special cause does not mean the worker should be blamed. The welder who had an exceptionally high number of weak welds was discovered to have defective equipment; the trucker with the most lost shipments had a complicated route with many more chances for misplaced packages; and the ineffective stockings factory worker needed glasses. Blaming the teachers of the two classrooms representing special-cause variation is the wrong place to start.

I started this chapter with the position that the control chart can help leaders out of the blaming and ranking spiral. Dr. Deming would have educators know that last in the ranking does not mean special cause. Only by creating control charts can one determine which results are special cause and which are common cause. Even when an entity falls outside the system on the negative side this does not mean the workers are at fault. It is often a result of a problem with equipment, materials, methods, or environment. A people problem is the last problem to study. Even though the two examples in the figures don't show special-cause variation on the positive side, the reader must recognize this possibility. Top rank does not mean special; it is an item beyond the control limit, on the positive side, that is to be studied to understand the success.

As an organization improves one classroom may exhibit special-cause variation when none existed before. Figure 20-3 documents one special-cause first grade classroom. Seven students missed more than 70 words on the 100-word story in a system where any more than four students is considered special cause. This classroom has been consistent in reading performance from

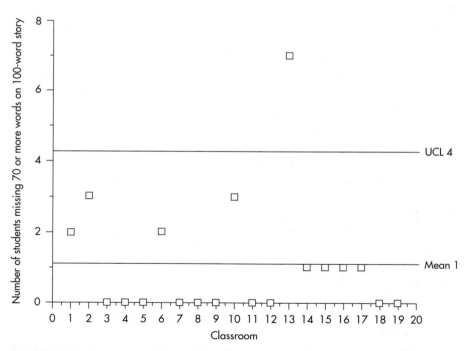

FIGURE 20-3. First grade reading control chart showing special-cause variation two years later.

year to year. The difference in 1995, however, is that a performance level that used to be within the system is now outside the system.

The other type of control chart for making judgments is the *p* (percent) chart. It is used when a percentage is to be plotted. Each item being examined is either OK or not OK/pass/fail, or some other binomial distribution. In Figure 20-4, a percentage of sad faces is plotted for each school. Faces are counted as sad or not sad.

The formula for the *p* chart is as follows:[6]

$$p = \text{percent}$$
$$\bar{p} = \text{average percent}$$
$$\text{UCL} = \bar{p} + 3\sqrt{\bar{p}(1-\bar{p}) \div n}$$
$$n = \text{total number tested}$$
$$\text{LCL} = \bar{p} - 3\sqrt{\bar{p}(1-\bar{p}) \div n}$$

The percentage of sad faces at each of six elementary schools, used as an example of the *p* control chart, is shown in Figure 20-4.

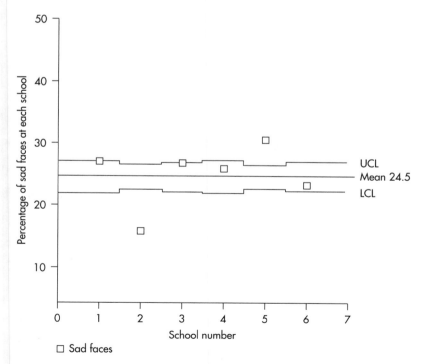

FIGURE 20-4. Control chart for sad face percentages.

Four of the schools are within the system. One school is above the system and one is below, meaning one school has a higher percentage of sad faces than limits of the system and one has fewer sad faces. When ranking data it can be determined which school is first and which is last, but nothing as useful as *above or below the system* is known. One school will always have the lowest percentage of sad faces and one will always have the highest percentage. These data alone are useless. The control chart, however, defines the system and shows which schools are above the system and which are below the system.

The *p* control chart in Figure 20-4 was produced a software package that generates accurate control charts, as was Figure 20-5. Figure 20-5 is a *c* chart, counting the number of referrals to the school office, by teacher, in a middle school. The system provides between 11 and 43 referrals per teacher. Ten teachers are above the system on the negative side, and 15 are below the LCL on the positive side. This is a system that statisticians would describe as being out of statistical control. First the system must be brought

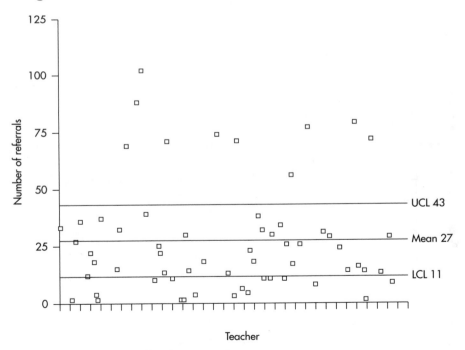

FIGURE 20-5.   Referrals to office showing special-cause variation.

under control, meaning all special, negative variation is eliminated and all other variation is brought within the system's limits. Then begins the hard work, improving the total system.

Table 20-1 displays the ranking of 41 states on the 1994 Fourth Grade Reading National Assessment of Educational Progress (NAEP). With this ranking Governor Pete Wilson of California has no data to tell him if his state is a special case requiring emergency educational surgery or if California is within the control limits of the American educational system and the last-place ranking is meaningless. Without knowledge of special- and common-cause variation he, along with the State Department of Education, panicked. They are probably guilty of mistake number one,[7] which is to "ascribe a variation to a special cause when in fact the cause belongs to the system (common cause)." Having a statistician at NAEP who understood common- and special-cause variation might have saved California millions of dollars in panicked spending to find the problem when probably no special cause existed. "Over-adjustment is a common example of mistake #1."[8]

The steps in using control charts are

1. Gather data. Often this is the same data that could be used for ranking.
2. If making a judgment decision at the conclusion of an event, compute either a *c* or a *p* chart. Use a *c* chart when there is no denominator and the raw count of occurrences is being plotted. Use a *p* chart when a percentage of data is being plotted and each item examined is binomial (for example, right/wrong; sad/not sad; red/not red).
3. Determine if one or more points are above the UCL or below the LCL. If so, there is special-cause variation.
4. If there is special-cause variation, work to eliminate it.
5. If all variation is common cause, work to reduce it; it can never be completely eliminated.

Quality proponents admonish leaders to think of control charts when ranked data are presented. Much is to be learned from control charts. Two additional examples emphasize this point. They are from the results of an examination given to 425 fourth

TABLE 20-1. Distribution of overall reading proficiency organized by average proficiency for the 1994 trial state reading assessment, grade four, public schools only.

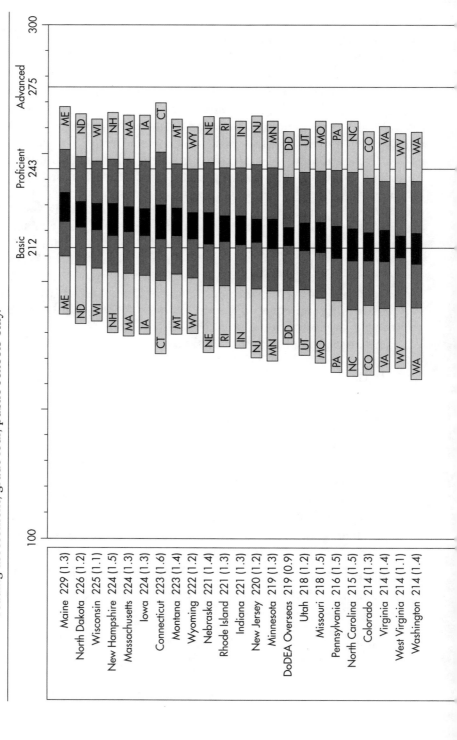

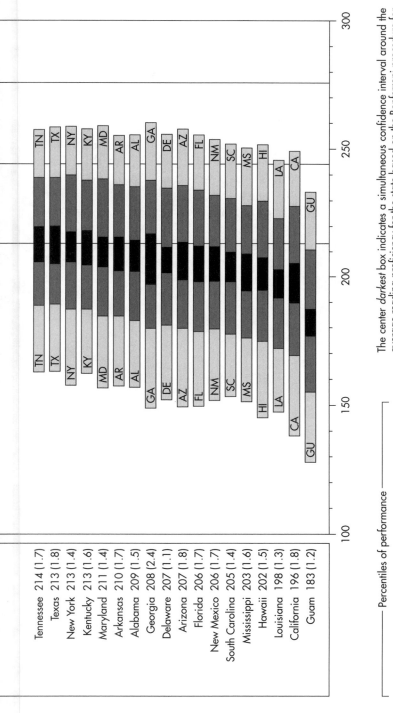

The center *darkest* box indicates a simultaneous confidence interval around the average reading proficiency for the state based on the Bonferroni procedure for multiple comparisons. The *darker shaded* boxes indicate the ranges between the 25th and 75th percentiles of the reading proficiency distribution. and the *lighter shaded* boxes the ranges between the 10th to 25th percentiles and the 75th to 90th percentiles of the distribution.

graders in six schools. Figure 20-6 displays the district mathematics system by item analysis. The average question was missed 107 times. The control chart further shows that on seven items the students excelled and on another seven items the students need significant help.

Figure 20-7 analyzes the data by gender instead of item. An average of 8 percent of the boys or the girls at each school missed 60 percent or more of the exam items. The LCL is 0 and the UCL is 15. All common-cause variation lies between 0 and 15 percent of the students. One case of special-cause variation exists: the girls on one campus. This principal and his staff are most curious to find out why!

The two control charts give educators much to address in the improvement and decision-making process. Ranking schools by test results would have provided no data with which to make important decisions.

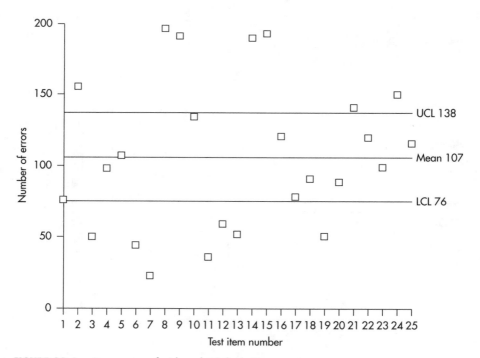

FIGURE 20-6. Item errors on fourth grade mathematics test.

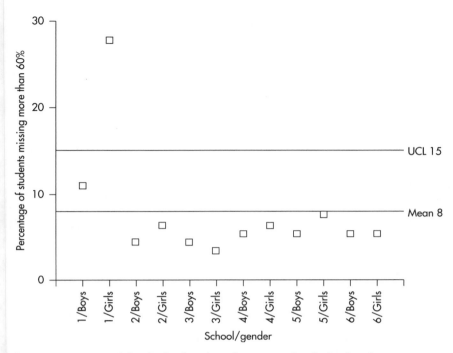

FIGURE 20-7. Control chart for fourth grade mathematics test, by school and gender.

Four control chart patterns appear from analysis of student learning. The first appears in Figure 20-8, which shows an out-of-control third grade mathematics system. The chart displays the percentage of students from each of 18 classrooms who met the 80 percent success criteria on a district mathematics exam. The range of students, in each classroom, meeting the success criteria is from 0 percent to 83 percent. The common-cause variation among the classrooms is between 21 percent and 50 percent, with special-cause variation both below and above the control limits. A system is out of control when it has special-cause variation. Five classrooms need significant help and four must be studied to learn reasons for their success. Parents should pay close attention to which classroom their students are assigned in this out-of-control system.

The second control chart pattern is also out of control, but special-cause variation is only on one side of the control limit. Figure 20-9 shows the number of students in each of 17 classrooms

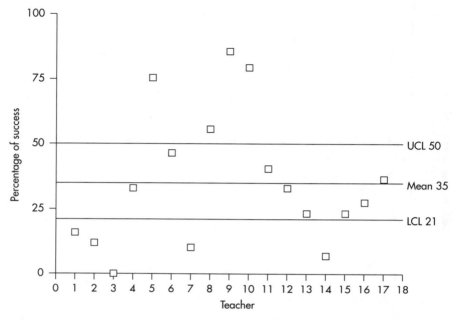

FIGURE 20-8.   Control chart, percentage of success for third grade mathematics.

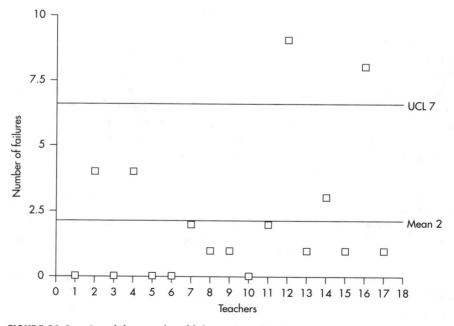

FIGURE 20-9.   Control chart, number of failures in second grade reading.

who experienced failure while reading a 100-word story. Failure was determined to be more than 30 errors on the story. The district system boundaries are from zero to seven students in each classroom making more than 30 errors. Between zero and seven students is considered common-cause variation. More than seven students is a special case; something unusual is happening in these classrooms. Two classrooms had special-cause variation with more failures than the district system. In this example, the district second grade reading system was working well enough to have no special-cause variation on the positive side. So many classrooms had one or no students experiencing reading failure that no classroom could be studied to determine the reasons for success.

The third pattern shows a system in control, which means there is no special-cause variation. Figure 20-10 shows the number of students from 16 classrooms who missed more than half of the questions on a fifth grade mathematics test. The system is in control, meaning that all variation is common cause; the variation is built into the district operations. Nevertheless, the system is not

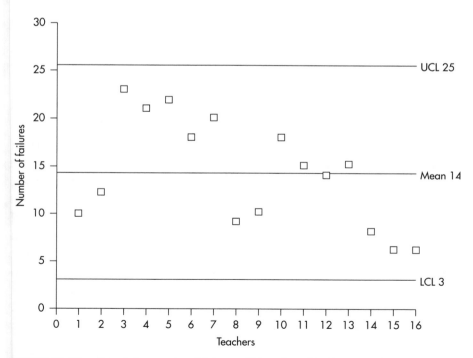

FIGURE 20-10. Control chart, number of failures in fifth grade mathematics.

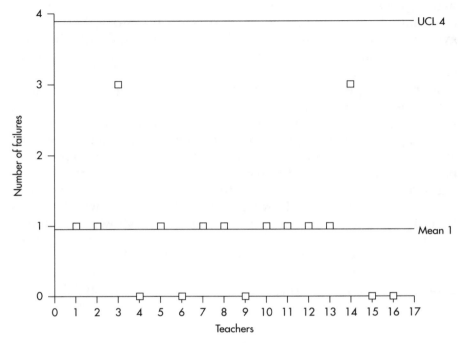

FIGURE 20-11.   Control chart, number of failures in third grade reading.

functioning well. There is a system problem to be solved by teachers and administrators.

The fourth pattern is desirable for all control charts. Figure 20-11 shows a system in control with positive results. It displays the number of third graders from 16 classrooms who missed more than 30 words on a 100-word story. The district system boundaries are from zero to four students in each room experiencing reading failure. All classrooms are between the UCL of four and the LCL of zero. Parents can feel comfortable having their student assigned to any of these classrooms; the system will deliver consistent quality in reading. The responsibility of everybody involved with third grade reading is to improve the instruction everywhere, with no focus on helping particular classrooms. The system can always be improved.

For more than 30 years I have seen statistical data on learning and often considered the expense and time necessary to collect the data a waste of resources. Nothing has come close to giving the picture of instruction that control charts can provide.

Notes

1. W. Edwards Deming, American Association of School Administrators Conference, Washington D.C., January 1992.
2. W. Edwards Deming, *Out of the Crisis* (Cambridge, Mass.: MIT Press, 1986), p. 337.
3. Ibid, p. 338.
4. Susan Leddick et al., *Improvement Tools for Education (K–12)* (Miamisburg, Ohio: PQ Systems, Inc., 1992).
5. Deming, *Out of the Crisis,* p. 256.
6. Ibid, p. 264.
7. Ibid, p. 318.
8. Ibid, p. 318.

Section VI

Eliminating Actions That Make Improving Student Learning Difficult

Yes, there are poor teachers; yes, there are terrible living conditions for many children; yes, there are administrators who should be fired; yes, unions represent employees and not children; yes . . . yes . . . yes. . . . Student learning can still be improved and students' enthusiasm for learning can still be maintained. This final section describes societal attitudes that hamper improved student learning. When teachers better understand these societal pressures, they will become more powerful leaders.

Chapter 21
LEGISLATIVE TAMPERING

Many people believe legislation makes society worse, but are at a loss to know why they feel this way. They can describe legislation that made a state or the nation worse, but cannot provide a theory as to why legislation makes it so. Dr. Deming provided the theory. Dr. Deming believed that almost all legislation is tampering: "Most legislation is correcting a mistake with another mistake."[1] Things get worse, not better, through tampering.

Dr. Deming's tampering model is described in several publications, but especially well by William Scherkenbach in *The Deming Road to Continual Improvement.* The materials necessary to demonstrate the tampering model are a funnel, a marble that will fall through the funnel, a large plain cloth, and a pen.

Dr. Deming would drop the marble through the funnel onto a target marked on the cloth. The marble would hit the target, and roll somewhere, and he would record the location where the marble stopped. He would repeat these steps 50 times with no adjustments to any of the variables. The location of the target, the height of the funnel, and the resting place of the marble prior to releasing it were kept constant for each of the 50 drops.

The 50 locations of the marble stops, each indicated by a dot on the cloth, make a circular pattern as shown in Figure 21-1.

The first 50 marble drops demonstrate that variation exists. After 50 or more drops one might have enough knowledge about marble drops to experiment with adjustments to reduce the size of

FIGURE 21-1. Normal variation without tampering. From *Deming's Road to Continual Improvement* by William W. Scherkenbach © 1991. Reprinted by permission of SPC Press, Inc., Knoxville, Tennessee.

the ring of dots around the target. The variation ring can never be eliminated, but means are available to reduce its size.

Impulsiveness creates tampering. A tampering manager has no patience to complete 50 drops before attempting improvements. Instead of considering slight variation from the target as normal and unavoidable, the tampering manager believes each movement away from the target is a special event that must not recur. Therefore, after each drop, and subsequent movement away from the target, the tampering manager adjusts the location of the funnel. This adjustment after each marble drop (like a new law) is an attempt to help the marble rest closer to the target, but, unfortunately, each adjustment (or new law) moves the marble further from the target. Even with the best of intentions, both the legislator and the tampering manager make things worse.

Dr. Deming had three means of moving the funnel, or tampering. Figure 21-2 shows the results of the first way to tamper. After each drop of the marble the tampering manager moves the funnel to compensate for the movement of the marble from the target. After each drop of the marble, the funnel is moved in the opposite direction of the marble's final resting place, the same distance by which the marble missed the last drop.

Figure 21-3 shows the second way to tamper. In this instance the target never moves. After each drop of the marble the tampering manager moves the funnel across the target to a spot opposite where the marble stopped on the last drop. The resulting error is even larger than with the steady aim for 50 tries or the first attempt at improvement.

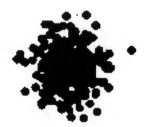

FIGURE 21-2. Tampering method 1. From *Deming's Road to Continual Improvement* by William W. Scherkenbach © 1991. Reprinted by permission of SPC Press, Inc., Knoxville, Tennessee.

FIGURE 21-3. Tampering method 2. From *Deming's Road to Continual Improvement* by William W. Scherkenbach © 1991. Reprinted by permission of SPC Press, Inc., Knoxville, Tennessee.

The third tampering method is shown in Figure 21-4, which, as Dr. Deming's put it, takes you to the "Milky Way." The first drop of the marble is aimed at the target as in the other methods. The second drop is made by placing the funnel directly over the location of the resting place of the first drop. Wherever the marble stops, this is the new target. Each successive drop of the marble is made by aiming for the resting place of the prior drop.

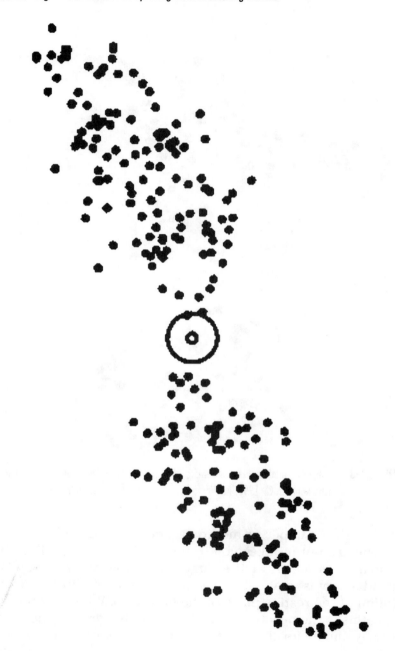

FIGURE 21-4. Tampering method 3. From *Deming's Road to Continual Improvement* by William W. Scherkenbach © 1991. Reprinted by permission of SPC Press, Inc., Knoxville, Tennessee.

From the perspective of the legislator, there are only two choices for legislation relating to schools: Do nothing or tamper. The electorate cannot stand doing nothing and since education doesn't have consistent data collected over many years, tampering is the only choice. To stop legislative tampering, education law must act like a system.

- Education law needs an aim. It has none.

- Education law must identify its customer. Who is the customer of the education law—the governor, the voters, the unions, the employees, other legislators, the media, or someone else?

- Education law focuses on the input to schools. This is quite silly, since the legislatures haven't established an aim. Almost all of the inputs are included in the financial laws. The mandated inputs are attendance, transportation, individual education plans for special education, gifted programs, bilingual services, food, labor negotiations, health care, remedial math and reading, and summer school.

- Education law often mandates processes. Republicans tend to mandate phonics as a reading process; Democrats tend to leave it up to schools to select their reading methods, but they mandate that more and more people are a protected class requiring diagnostic or prescriptive documentation. Both political parties tamper equally. Without a legislative aim, state and federal legislators do their best. They pass laws that cause school districts to go in opposite directions at the same time. A federal example is the GOALS 2000 and I.D.E.A. programs. School districts are forced to spend less money on the goal to be number one in math and science so they can afford special education attorneys.

- Education law never has, to the best of my knowledge, accepted the viewpoint that taxpayers should pay for output, not for input. If they did pay for output, however, the federal government would no longer loan money to poor students to attend college (input), but would instead reimburse colleges when these students graduated (output). This income would be used by colleges to provide scholarships for future students currently living in poverty. With output legislation, the colleges will be taking the risks. If the colleges provide scholarships to students who don't graduate, the colleges lose, not the taxpayers.

• Education law has no quality measurement. Legislation measurement still focuses on ranking, punishing low-performing schools, and rewarding high-performing schools. No data are available to know if these laws resulted in improvement.

Education legislation must become a system and it must stop tampering. The following are examples of system thinking in an education legislation system.

1. *An aim for education legislation:* Produce high school graduates who meet specific standards.

2. *A customer for education law:* The customer is local school districts. The purpose of all legislation is to help school districts produce more graduates who meet the standards. The state legislators set the standards for which they will pay, and the Congress sets the standards for which it will reimburse.

3. *Helping school district staff work with supply:* Use the legislative process to help all of society better prepare children for school success. Investments are necessary for libraries, health, and recreational agencies to improve the supply to schools.

4. *Input laws:* Beyond safety and health, school districts need only financial input. Legislators must use their wisdom to eliminate existing laws that act as barriers to student improvement.

5. *Process:* It is not up to the legislature to determine educational processes.

6. *Output:* The legislature has every reason to demand accurate output information. How many dropouts did the state produce? How many graduates are prepared for work? How many graduates are prepared for university admission? Legislatures should pay only for output plus safety and health mandates. State departments of education can be funded based on the number of graduates (output) in the state. Once departments of education recognize that the following year's budget is based on the number of graduates who meet the state standards, they will treat school districts like valued customers instead of promoting the current inspector-inspectee relationship.

7. *Quality measurement:* The legislature needs to know, based on output, which school districts fall above the system, within the system, and below the system. Those districts above the system

need to be studied to discover reasons for their success, and those below the system must be helped. Legislatures must understand that being last in the ranking does not equal *below the system*. A school with 49 percent dropouts is most likely within the system if other districts have 48.7 percent, 48.6 percent, 48.4 percent, and 48.3 percent dropouts. Control charts determine precisely which schools are within, below, and above the system. The legislature doesn't have to like the system; nevertheless, the state system is producing schools like these. On the other hand, if a school has 49 percent dropouts and the next closest schools have 34 percent, 33.5 percent, 33.2 percent, and 33.1 percent dropouts, this school may be below the system and need special help. The control charts in Chapter 20 could be valuable for decision making in legislatures and state departments of education.

Improving the system through these seven elements is far superior to the normal inclination to hire more inspectors when there is a quality problem, or as Dr. Deming said, "Put on more inspectors. This is a commonly accepted reaction to a problem in quality—a sure road to more trouble."[2]

Having an aim for the system can also help resolve some of the most divisive educational topics. Not long ago, my wife and I were dining with two friends: one an educator employed by a Christian organization and the other an executive director of a state school boards association. One of them said, "I think vouchers would help education." The immediate reply was, "In my lifetime, this state's tax money will never be sent to Rome." So much for establishing the boundaries of discussion.

A few minutes into the discussion, I offered a solution: "What if school districts were paid only for producing graduates?" I explained that each state can easily compute the current cost to produce each high school graduate. This cost is determined by dividing one year's total education investment by the total number of graduates. If school districts were paid only for producing graduates, the local school board would be able to allocate its resources in any way it desired to produce more graduates. It could even use some of its money to send students to private schools. The board would be using all available resources to produce more graduates who meet state requirements so that it could collect state revenues. The school board would recognize that it would be paid nothing for each dropout.

I explained to my guests that I didn't mean to say educators are money hungry and will only work for better education if they are paid more. Most educators I know are motivated by doing what is best for students. Organizations, however, must meet payroll and will organize themselves to maximize income.

Both of our friends agreed that paying only for graduates has possibilities, even though details would have to be worked out. Paying school districts for graduates might not be the answer to the voucher battle, but until all agree on an aim for K–12 education and then legislate to accomplish the aim, elected officials will continue to tamper. At the very least education should be able to document that the cost to produce a graduate is coming down.

Just like the bowls of water under Panamanian bedposts, legislative tampering is everywhere. Dr. Deming's thinking is clear regarding how this nation and its states can help educators improve student learning, rather than continually making it more difficult.

Notes

1. W. Edwards Deming, American Association of School Administrators Conference, Washington, D.C., January 1992.
2. W. Edwards Deming, *Out of the Crisis* (Cambridge, Mass.: MIT Press, 1986), p. 29.

Chapter 22

THE INANE DESIRE FOR ONLY ONE NUMBER

I was reminded of people's inane desire for a single number while I was speaking with a local realtor. He shared what he thought was a compliment: The district of which I am superintendent was the third-best district in the county. (Shasta County, California, has 26,000 pupils and 25 school districts ranging in size from 50 to 4500.) Never had I seen any data in any educational or public documents that would warrant a single number for a district and thus enable such a ranking. Nevertheless, he was very confident in his *one* number.

The Kentucky Reform Education Act encoded the one-number concept into its revolutionary legislation. Each school in the state is expected to have a score of 100 within 20 years. The score is arrived at by combining all scores on all measurements into one grand number.[1]

Combining all the scores, however, just creates mud. Mud is composed of at least soil and water. Chemists can easily describe the elements that combine to form the water, the soil, and whatever else is in the mud. On their own, the water, soil, and other substances can be understood. But when combined into one test tube, it looks like mud.

The same is true when educational numbers are combined. The equation looks something like this: Reading + Writing + Spelling + Mathematical Problem Solving + Mathematical Concepts + Scientific Literacy + Scientific Problem Solving + Geography + History Assessments = Mud

In a blaming society, creating mud makes perfect sense. Otherwise, what would we sling? When each school or school district is given one and only one number, everybody can set about blaming each other for any ranking they don't desire. If there are data for each subject, however, the message is different: All can improve.

The now-defunct California Learning Assessment System test in California made many excellent improvements in assessment. The combination of data, however, was one of its mistakes. In mathematics students were scored on eight math concept questions (information) and two math problem-solving questions (knowledge). The statisticians hired by the California Department of Education combined the two scores into one score. A 3-by-9 matrix was built with a cell for each possible score (0 to 8 on information and 0 to 2 on knowledge). Each student was assigned a score from 1 to 6. A zero on both information and knowledge resulted in a score of 1. A score of 8 on information and 2 on knowledge resulted in a score of 6. In between, however, there were a variety of ways to earn a score of 1, 2, 3, 4, or 5. Those receiving the results didn't know where to begin improvement. The muddy results were useless because two valuable pieces of data (information and knowledge) were unnecessarily combined. When improvement is the educational goal, mud is of no value.

The webs described in Chapter 11 are an answer to the one-number dilemma. Instead of one number for a school, improvement can be displayed on two webs printed side by side on one sheet of paper. Looking with frustration through report after report to understand a school is what leads to the one-number concept. The web can end the frustration of multiple reports.

Ideally student progress would also be reported on a student web. Figure 22-1 is a proposed student report card web that would help students and parents see a bigger picture of student learning. I envision the web as the cover of the student portfolio.

Each subject has one diameter on the web; the top radius is for knowledge measured on a continuum and the bottom radius is the information measured by counting. Note, however, that not all subjects are represented on the web; the figure is merely a concept, not a final product. Clearly the most difficult aspect of having such a student report card is getting communities to agree on the knowledge and information to be learned by transition grades such as 5, 8, and 12. Once this is determined, students can be assessed at year's end and an appropriate dot placed on all radii. Connecting the dots, using a different color for each school year, will easily communicate to parents and students the progress in learning.

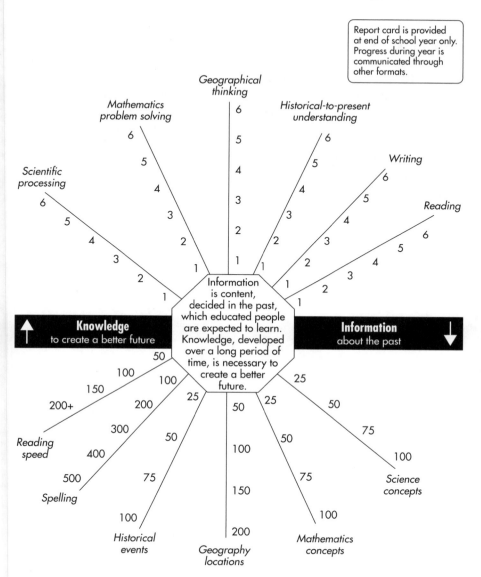

The ends of the radii on the student report card web represent the level of knowledge and information expected at the end of grade five. Information is measured like a track-and-field event: by counting. Knowledge is measured like a gymnastics event: by measuring against a continuum, from lowest to highest quality.

FIGURE 22-1. Student report card web.

The student web description is written in the future tense; I have not yet witnessed its implementation. It does seem, however, that the student web is the next logical step and that it is one answer to the disease of one-number-itis. Certainly the field of psychology is helping educators with advancements such as Multiple Intelligences and The Structure of the Intellect. The student web is a way for educators to communicate individual strengths, gifts, and types of intelligence. Even though this is a concept yet to be implemented, it is true that all children are unique and, thus, each web will be unique. Instead of educational mud there can be beautiful, multicolored, unique webs for every student.

Note

1. W. Edwards Deming, *Out of the Crisis* (Cambridge, Mass.: MIT Press, 1986).

Chapter 23
THE STATUS QUO

To the outside observer it is almost impossible to imagine why education looks so much the same or, why the many pockets of outstanding education seemingly cannot become the norm for every student, every year. Why, with all of the clamor for change, do public schools resist change? Perhaps a more important question is, *Why are schools so effective in avoiding change?* The third force interferring with improved student learning is the status quo.

The force-field analysis is the perfect quality tool to display status quo. Force-field theory states that status quo occurs when the forces in favor of improvement are equal to the forces opposed to improvement. Every teacher I know can identify with that statement. One of the most significant messages to leaders from the force-field analysis is they don't need to create the desire for improvement; it is already present within every organization. The job of leaders is to remove the forces working against improvement so that the forces in favor of improvement that already exist can go to work. This may be why Dr. Deming stated that change is more listening than selling.[1] It takes a lot of listening to understand the forces opposed to improvement. Examples of driving forces in favor of improvement follow.

Educators who desire to provide for children, either what was provided for them, or what they wish was provided for them, are abundant. They work in every school with enthusiasm. The driving forces within these teachers are listed in Figure 23-1. They know how to respond to the varied needs of students and parents; they learn every day and know that some criticism is valid. So, if this is true, the question remains, *Why are schools so shackled by the status quo? What forces could possibly be supporting status quo?*

In typical conversations, the five themes in Figure 23-2 are frequently cited as the forces that keep the wall of the status quo in place. Remember that there is great pressure to eliminate the status quo. An equal, opposite, and powerful pressure must be in place to

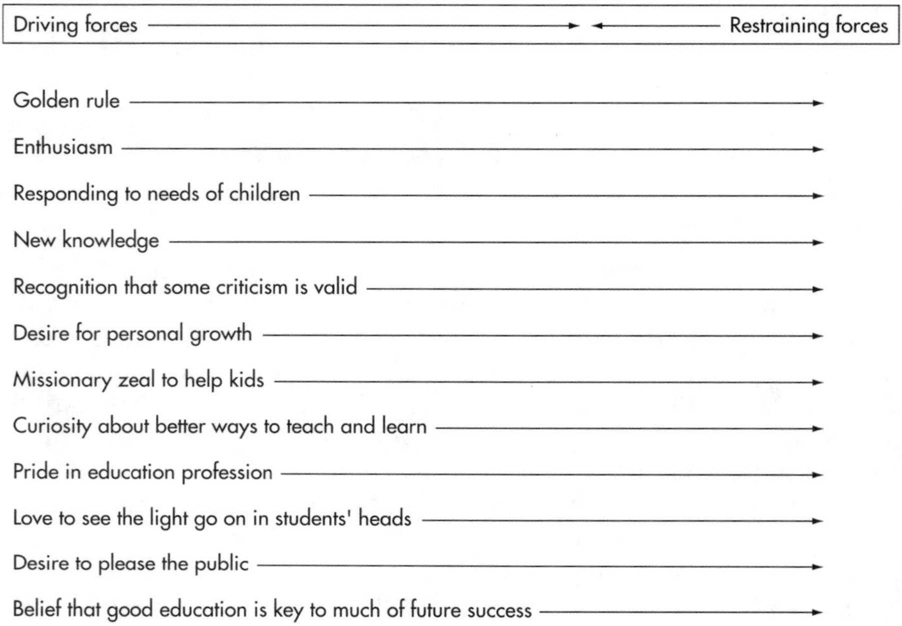

Driving forces ⟶ ⟵ Restraining forces

Golden rule ⟶
Enthusiasm ⟶
Responding to needs of children ⟶
New knowledge ⟶
Recognition that some criticism is valid ⟶
Desire for personal growth ⟶
Missionary zeal to help kids ⟶
Curiosity about better ways to teach and learn ⟶
Pride in education profession ⟶
Love to see the light go on in students' heads ⟶
Desire to please the public ⟶
Belief that good education is key to much of future success ⟶

FIGURE 23-1. Forces in favor of improved student learning.

Driving forces ⟶ ⟵ Restraining forces

⟵ Tenure
⟵ Lack of private sector competition
⟵ Unions
⟵ Education establishment
⟵ Poor parenting

FIGURE 23-2. Possible forces opposed to improved student learning.

keep the wall standing. Quality thinking, however, rejects these five themes as forces powerful enough to keep the status quo in place. Dr. Deming stated that 94 percent of the problems of any organization are caused by the system and only 6 percent by the people within the organization.[2] He saw these five themes as part of the 6 percent. Thus, if all states abolish tenure, every school has private sector competition, unions are abolished, parents discipline their children appropriately, and educators stop their influence peddling in the capitols, 6 percent of the support for the status quo would be removed. Admittedly, the wall would have a few blocks removed, but getting it to fall over is wishful thinking. Like many educators I am in favor of eliminating the divisiveness of unions; I believe that case law has made tenure obstructive; and now that I'm a grand-parent I know a fair amount about parenting. Nevertheless, 6 percent is the number to remember. A few missing blocks in the wall of the status quo won't suffice.

In 1995 I had a conversation with a minister regarding the mis-erable state of the private school at his church. The school had class sizes of 15 or fewer students, a 20-year history, boring cur-riculum (in the words of the pastor), and negative teachers (again, according to the pastor). Parents of 12 of the 15 students in one classroom had been told by the teacher that their children had attention deficit disorder. Ironically, this school had no tenure, no union, was not affected by the educational establishment, com-peted in the free market economy, and the parents generally knew how to discipline their children. None of the five common reasons for the status quo were present, and yet the school was in terrible shape.

Dr. Deming wrote, "A single unexplained failure of a theory requires modification or even abandonment of the theory."[3] So, according to Dr. Deming, either the five themes explaining school failure are incomplete, and thus need major modification, or they are not the actual buttresses supporting the wall after all.

If these five commonly held beliefs are not at work, what is supporting the status quo? Dr. Deming named 14 supports in his book *Out of the Crisis.* They are displayed on the force-field analysis in Figure 23-3.[4] (Note that the driving forces and the restraining forces are not lined up with each other as opposites.)

It takes tremendous effort to keep the status quo in education. In fact, people become very tired of working hard and seeing only the status quo. I'd say that many of the restraining and driving forces in education are blowing at hurricane levels. Everybody is pushing hard. It's a classic stalemate that will persist until the focus is shifted away from the five themes in Figure 23-2. Once this happens and the real restraining forces are eliminated, the powerful driving forces will take education to new heights. Dr. Deming's 14

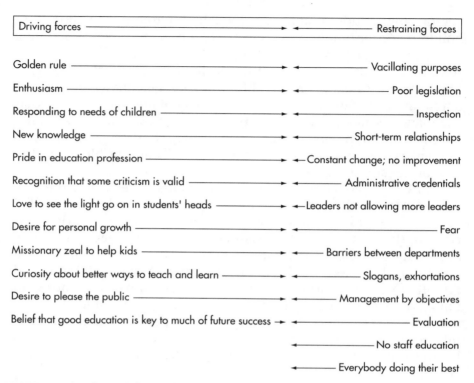

FIGURE 23-3.   The real restraining forces against improved student learning.

points stand ready to remove the restraining forces. They are as follows (I have taken the liberty to rephrase them for education and connections to other chapters):

1. **Create constancy of purpose.** Year after year, relentlessly pursue the same standards of excellence. Eliminate vacillating purposes, often known as the *flavor of the month.*

2. **Adopt the new philosophy.** Accept the fact that few educational problems are caused by people working within the system. Most are system problems that only leaders of states (governors), leaders of districts (superintendents), leaders of schools (principals), and leaders of classrooms (teachers) can remove. Substitute leadership for poor laws, regulations, and rules. Superintendents cannot change laws, teachers cannot change regulations, and

students cannot change teachers' rules. Leadership is needed by those with the power to change the systems for which they are responsible.

3. Stop trying to inspect quality into education. It has never worked and never will. The millions of dollars now spent on educational inspectors should be invested in the implementation of Dr. Deming's quality philosophy.

4. Build long-term relationships of trust and loyalty with suppliers (parents and others working with preschool children), stakeholders (parents), and customers (children).

5. Never stop improving. Define improvement in every aspect of schooling and continually show progress.

6. Train all employees in quality. Stop requiring administrative credentials that perpetuate management by objective.

7. Institute leadership. Leaders must lead the improvement process instead of criticizing others' mistakes. Leaders create more leaders.

8. Stop using fear as the major tool to control students. *If you don't do your homework, you'll get an F.*

9. Break down barriers between subsystems in education—preschool versus elementary school versus middle school versus high school versus community college versus university versus support staff versus teachers versus counselors versus nurses versus administrators versus board members.

10. Eliminate management by objective. In a school district, each principal can meet his or her objectives, but the organizational team will be torn apart because everyone is going in opposite directions. Substitute constancy of purpose.

11. Eliminate numerical quotas (such as, number one in the world in math and science). Note that webs have no quotas. They only have a direction toward less failure and more success. Any movement toward more success and less failure, no matter how small, is improvement.

12. Help everyone have pride in their work. Stop the demoralizing evaluation process, which discourages students and makes adults feel like they are in school again.

13. Learn about everything (education), not just how to do the job better (training).

14. Use everybody's help to transform the organization. Stop thinking, "If everybody would only do their best we'd be transformed."

The force-field analysis is designed to help decision makers understand the forces working against each other to prop up the status quo. The analysis will work in any organization or occupation. As a tool, the force-field analysis was designed to be left blank, with volunteers filling in both the left and right fields from their observations. Dr. Deming, however, described a complete set of forces working against improvement. Some of the 14 forces might not be apparent in a given situation, but using his list can be more helpful than trying to construct restraining forces out of the blue. Figure 23-4 shows a force-field analysis and 14-point check sheet combined into one tool.

The lesson to be learned from the force-field analysis is that no matter how hard one pushes to bring about improvement through added pressure to driving forces, the status quo will remain. All restraining forces have the power to subdue the strongest driving forces. Sometimes the restraining forces go underground, but as soon as the boss changes, there's the old status quo again. The only way to allow the driving forces to take hold permanently is to remove, not what appears to be the restraining forces (the five themes), but the root causes of the restraint. Dr. Deming's 14 points are the root causes. And, I am sad to say, these roots are deep down in the dry soil of American education; there is no quick fix.

Driving forces ——————————————▶ ◀—————————— Restraining forces

Is the organization plagued with. . .

——————————▶ ◀———————————————————— Vacillating purposes?

——————————▶ ◀———————————————— Blaming people for system problems?

——————————▶ ◀——————————————— Trying to inspect quality in?

——————————▶ ◀—Making decisions on price only? No work with customers and suppliers?

——————————▶ ◀——————————————— Never knowing if changes improve anything?

——————————▶ ◀————————————————————— No on-the-job training?

——————————▶ ◀——————————————— Leaders not helping people improve?

——————————▶ ◀——————— Teachers, support staff, and administrators who manage by fear?

——————————▶ ◀——————————————— Barriers between departments?

——————————▶ ◀——————————————— Slogans and exhortations?

——————————▶ ◀——————————————————— Numerical goals?

——————————▶ ◀——————— Barriers that rob people of pride in workmanship?

——————————▶ ◀——————————————— Lack of education opportunities?

——————————▶ ◀——————————— Only a few who care about transforming to quality?

FIGURE 23-4. Deming's 14 points on a force-field analysis.

Notes

1. W. Edwards Deming, American Association of School Administrators Conference, Washington, D.C., January 1992.
2. W. Edwards Deming, *The New Economics* (Cambridge, Mass.: MIT Press, 1993).
3. Ibid, p. 107.
4. *The Memory Jogger for Education* (Methuen, Mass.: Goal/QPC, 1992), p. 73.

CONCLUSION

In the 1970s an error occurred on the SAT which was both embarrassing to the Educational Testing Service and joyful to the student who discovered the mistake. The question asked students how many faces a new polyhedron would have after it was formed by touching one face of a tetrahedron to one face of a pyramid with a square base. The test question stipulated that the faces on the tetrahedron and the triangular faces of the pyramid were congruent. The correct answer is five faces; the answer programmed into SAT's computer was seven.

Seven seems like the obvious answer; the tetrahedron has four faces and the pyramid has five faces for a total of nine faces. If two faces are eliminated by touching them together, there should be seven faces on the new polyhedron. This, however, is wrong. The two polyhedra come together in a most delightful way to create a polyhedra imagined by few. None of the experts hired by SAT visualized the correct answer of five faces.

Figure C-1 shows a pyramid and tetrahedron that can be copied, cut out, and taped together to see the five faces. Eight of the nine faces are labeled; on the last face write the name of the school district you care about the most. The tetrahedron represents a school district with three divisions; instruction, personnel, and business. These units manage the district's resources—its ideas, its people, and its physical assets. The pyramid represents Dr. Deming's concept of profound knowledge. Any one of the four disciplines of profound knowledge can connect with any of the three district divisions or the organization as a whole. When this coupling becomes the norm, the organization operates at a level seen by few.

The name Dr. Deming gave to this level of organization is *fourth generation management*. The four levels of organization are

- Level 1. I'll do it myself.
- Level 2. Do it the way I tell you.

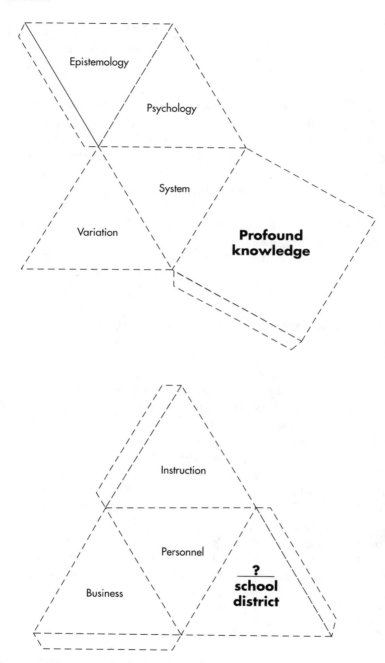

FIGURE C-1.   Pyramid with a square base and a tetrahedron to assemble.

- Level 3. Management by objectives.
- Level 4. Common aim with all resources directed toward accomplishing the aim through teamwork.

It is only at level 4 that leaders can transform their organization.

Governors can operate at level 4 by designating that K–12 districts be the agency responsible for the quality of high school graduates and focusing the efforts of all other educational agencies toward helping K–12 districts improve student learning. All laws that obstruct the accomplishment of this aim should be repealed. In all states where current law divides the responsibility for education among several agencies, the governors must change the structure. Governors must not sign legislation that has their departments of education dealing with individual schools. If agencies are created between the state and the districts, it must be made clear that these agencies only exist to help K–12 districts produce quality high school graduates. These agencies serve to please their customers—the districts—not to carry out gubernatorial mandates.

Superintendents can operate at level 4 by helping their communities determine the quality of graduates they desire and organizing the competing factions so they work together to accomplish the aim. They must not rank or otherwise destroy any portion of their system. Everybody must know how their work helps accomplish the aim. Business staffs are responsible every year for reducing expenses that do not add value to the education of students. This leaves more resources for education. Personnel staffs are responsible every year to improve the quality of staff working with students through better hiring procedures, staff development, and documentation of poor performance when necessary. Many other employees are responsible for the health and safety of students while at school. Superb work on their part enables instructional staff to accomplish their aim.

Principals can operate at level 4 by helping parents, students, and staffs work together to accomplish their portion of the aim. Since few schools encompass grades K–12, all school staffs must see how and where they fit into the aim of helping society gain more outstanding high school graduates. They must model for everyone that schools are not managed by fear when operating at level 4. When everybody understands the aim, has input into changing the aim when necessary, and has continual feedback on school accomplishment, fear is necessary in only the most severe cases of poor behavior.

Teachers, for whom this book is written, can operate at level 4 by seeing their classrooms and their students' parents as a community of learners moving together toward the accomplishment of academic and maturation goals. They must not think of their classes as groups of individuals to be ranked, rewarded, punished, or extrinsically motivated. The purpose of *Improving Student Learning* is to describe what is necessary for teachers to operate at level 4. Even though teachers are central to improved student learning, they cannot do it alone. Teachers need superlative leadership from their principals, superintendents, state superintendents, and governors.

Appendix A
DIRECTIONS TO FOURTH, FIFTH, AND SIXTH GRADE TEACHERS REGARDING GEOGRAPHY

Introduction
A basic portion of a good education in geography is knowing locations of major cities, states, countries, continents, mountains, oceans, rivers, and deserts. In order to increase student success in geography, Enterprise educators have combined efforts to create the attached documents and directions.

Aim
For Enterprise students to know 300 locations in Shasta County, California, the United States, and the World by the end of sixth grade.

How were the locations chosen?
The locations were selected by Enterprise teachers under the leadership of Arlene Oleiri-Johnson, grade four; Damon Cropsey, grade five; and Harold Silva, grade six.

What free materials are available?
Three different laminated maps are available for Enterprise teachers. The fourth grade maps have 100 locations, the fifth grade maps have 200 locations, and the sixth grade maps have 300 locations. One map is available for each student. In addition, teachers may request dice from B. J. Olson. They are used for randomly selecting locations during quizzes. The dice are 100 sided, 0–1, and

0–1–2. Fourth grade teachers only need a 100-sided die to select one number from the list of 100 locations. Fifth grade teachers need a 100-sided die along with the die that has three zeros and three ones. Both dice are thrown. The smaller die tells the teacher whether to select a location from the fourth grade list or the fifth grade list. The 100-sided die tells which location from a particular list. Sixth grade teachers need a die with 0–1–2 because they are selecting from three different lists.

What data should be kept?

The most important data is a year-end quiz. The results tell the teacher what number of students learned 90 percent to 100 percent of the locations, 80 percent to 89 percent of the locations, and so on. This is baseline data to be used to compare the results from the next year's class. The purpose of the histogram is to create a better future, which means each succeeding year fewer students will score at the left of the histogram and more at the right.

What about ongoing weekly data?

The recommended method for tracking weekly progress is a quiz on 10 items in fourth grade, 14 items in fifth grade, and 17 items in sixth grade. The items are randomly selected at the time of the quiz, thus eliminating cramming. The results are recorded as a class run chart, class scatter diagram, and student run charts. The computer program is available from Dan Williams, our district technology coordinator. The purpose of the ongoing data collection is to adjust teaching strategies throughout the year to improve the quality of learning by year's end.

What is the most common error made recording weekly data?

The most common error is recording the average items correct for a class rather than the total number correct. In the beginning this seems to make sense because the average doesn't diminish when several students are absent. The negative side of recording average, however, is that 50 percent of the students will notice on their individual run chart they are below average—not a good message when they need to be encouraged to learn all locations. Experience has shown that more than half of the students will learn all locations by the end of the year. Thus, a student with one error the last week of school would receive a below-average message—not the memory we want to create.

Are the dice necessary?

No. There are other ways to randomly select the locations. Dan can provide you with random-number lists or show you how to use Excel to create your own lists. You may also write the locations on small cards and have students draw a location from a hat. Both of these methods are quicker than the dice because it takes so long for the 100-sided die to stop rolling.

How are teachers dealing with absences?

One way is to do nothing. The class run chart shows a dip in progress because of absences. This is true in all occupations; production goes down when people are absent. The other way is to have students give each other the quizzes they missed during recess and lunch periods. Students do appreciate a complete run chart with no breaks.

How often should students have data updated?

As soon as possible after each quiz, because the data are helpful in planning future learning activities.

Does having a list of 300 locations indicate a district desire for students to learn by memorization and rote drill?

No. Most of what people know they learned through experiences. For example, people reading this know the location of Sacramento. They did not memorize Sacramento, but had experiences that gave them this knowledge. It is hoped that students will have rich, interesting, meaningful geographical or historical experiences that will implant the locations permanently in their brains. No message is being delivered that students are to memorize (and forget) these locations. Our aim, *Maintain enthusiasm while increasing learning,* is as important in geography as any other subject. Students can learn these 300 locations while they maintain their natural desire for learning about other places.

RUBRIC FOR HUMAN BODY PAPER

There are many systems that work together in the human body. You are to write a paper showing your knowledge of these systems and how they work within the human body. You will write this paper four different times and as we go through the human body system in class, your knowledge on this topic should show growth each time you write the paper. On the following page you will find the scoring criteria by which the quality of your paper will be assessed.

8	**Exceptional achievement.** Has mastered knowledge of subject. *Information is authoritative and encompasses knowledge of all body systems, using proper scientific terms.				
7	**Distinguished achievement.** Authority on subject. *Information is authoritative and interesting with many scientific terms used in describing all of the body systems.				
6	**Noteworthy achievement.** Knowledgeable and interesting. *Information of many systems is described in a focused and consistent manner.				
5	**Satisfactory achievement.** Informative, but unfocused. *Information shows the writer is interested in the topic, but is general, using few scientific terms and missing some of the systems.				
4	**Some indication of achievement.** General. *Information is portrayed as important, but less informative than a 5. General statements are made about some of the systems rather than specifics, which shows lack of knowledge.				
3	**Limited indication of achievement.** Undeveloped, unspecific. *Information of many systems is missing. Those that are mentioned are briefly explained.				
2	**Few indications of achievement.** Uninformative. *Information is very general and badly organized. Very few systems are mentioned, let alone explained.				
1	**Inappropriate response.** Off topic.				
	TOTAL				

Ken Banner, science teacher, developed this rubric for his eighth grade science classes. The data he collected over a quarter of the year are included in Chapter 8, "Measuring Knowledge."

ANALYTIC SCORING GUIDES

Analytic Scoring Scale		
Understanding the Problem	**0:**	Complete misunderstanding of the problem.
	1:	Part of the problem misunderstood or misinterpreted.
	2:	Complete understanding of the problem.
Planning a Solution	**0:**	No attempt, or totally inappropriate plan.
	1:	Partially correct plan based on part of the problem being interpreted correctly.
	2:	Plan could have led to a correct solution if implemented properly.
Getting an Answer	**0:**	No answer, or wrong answer based on an inappropriate plan.
	1:	Copying error; computational error; partial answer for a problem with multiple answers.
	2:	Correct answer and correct label for the answer.

Source: NCTM, *How to Evaluate Progress in Problem Solving*, 1987. Used with permission.

Focused Holistic Scoring Point Scale

---

0 Points

These papers have one of the following characteristics:
- They are blank.
- The data in the problem may be simply recopied, but nothing is done with the data or there is work but no apparent understanding of the problem.
- There is an incorrect answer and no other work is shown.

1 Point

These papers have one of the following characteristics:
- There is a start toward finding the solution beyond just copying data that reflects some understanding, but the approach used would not have led to a correct solution.
- An inappropriate strategy is started but not carried out, and there is no evidence that the student turned to another strategy. It appears that the student tried one approach that did not work and then gave up.
- The student tried to reach a subgoal but never did.

2 Points

These papers have one of the following characteristics:
- The student used an inapproproate strategy and got an incorrect answer, but the work showed some understanding of the problem.
- An appropriate strategy was used, but—
  a) it was not carried out far enough to reach a solution (e.g., there were only 2 entries in an organized list);
  b) it was implemented incorrectly and thus led to no answer or an incorrect answer.
- The student successfully reached a subgoal, but went no further.
- The correct answer is shown, but—
  a) the work is not understandable;
  b) no work is shown.

3 Points

These papers have one of the following characteristics:
- The student has implemented a solution strategy that could have led to the correct solution, but he or she misunderstood part of the problem or ignored a condition in the problem.

Focused Holistic Scoring Point Scale—Continued

---

3 Points (continued)

- Appropriate solution strategies were properly applied, but—
  a) the student answered the problem incorrectly for no apparent reason;
  b) the correct numerical part of the answer was given and the answer was not labeled or was labeled incorrectly;
  c) no answer is given.
- The correct answer is given, and there is some evidence that appropriate solution strategies were selected. However, the implementation of the strategies is not completely clear.

4 Points

These papers have one of the following characteristics:
- The student made an error in carrying out an appropriate solution strategy. However, this error does not reflect misunderstanding of either the problem or how to implement the strategy, but rather it seems to be a copying or computational error.
- Appropriate strategies were selected and implemented. The correct answer was given in terms of the data in the problem.

Source: National Academy Press, *Measuring Up*, 1993. Used with permission.

READING SCORING GUIDE

Score   **Description**

6 . . . . **Exciting, engaging, interesting, well written, technically correct**

This reader not only answers questions accurately but also makes sensitive, insightful connections that give the reader the impression that this is a quality reader.

5 . . . . **Very good, technically correct, engaging, and interesting**

This student answers questions accurately and has made some sensitive connections to the piece of literature. The response does not, however, indicate any particular deep insight into the work.

4 . . . . **A full and technically correct answer, with connection**

This reader has made a technically correct answer and has made some attempt to add some connection to the piece of literature. It is not particularly engaging, somewhat flat, and matter-of-fact. But the connection is noted and the question answered. This reader would be considered an average reader and reading and responding at grade level.

3 . . . . **A technically correct answer, no overt connection offered**

This reader merely answered the question, which is technically correct, but makes no attempt to show that he or she made any connection. This reader would be considered slightly below reading level.

2 . . . . **A limited answer**

This reader's answer lacks details. There is, however, an attempt to answer the question, which makes it a limited attempt. With a little more effort, this student could rise to a level 3.

1 . . . . **No attempt to answer**

Answers like, "I don't know" or "Who cares?" fall into this category.

Reading knowledge scoring guide used by teacher Guy Piché in his seventh grade classes.

WRITING SCORING GUIDE

6 . . . . **All of 5 and more**

This is an extraordinary piece of writing for this grade level; it clearly is exceptional, both on a mechanical and contextual level. The piece stands alone as inspiration and rare. Few 6s are given throughout the year. It truly is a prize that should be sought by young writers.

5 . . . . **All of 4 and more**

This piece of writing displays risk-taking in sentence structure, word usage, or mechanics, such as the use of new vocabulary words or uncommon punctuation like the semicolon, colon, hyphen, or dash.

Goes beyond the mere writing task, explores the topic on a personal or environmental level. A feeling of sincerity is evident, or at least an attempt to do so is. A sentence or short phrase, some bit of wisdom could qualify for this.

4 . . . . **At grade level**

Writing task completed

Mini-essay format/essay format/some structures noted

Attempted to display a reasonable command of basic mechanics (punctuation, capitalization, spelling, sentence structure, and editing skills)

Displays appropriate vocabulary and usage skills

3 . . . . **Slightly below grade level**

Student might have a basic command of the mini-essay format but lacks one or more basic mechanical skills

2 . . . . **Serious organizational and or mechanical problems**

Could be a display of a lack of effort as well

1 . . . . **Apathetic statement**

"I don't know," "Who cares," "Don't know"

Writing scoring guide used by teacher Guy Piché in his seventh grade classes.

INDEX

14 points, of Deming, 219–22

A

Action, in PDSA cycle, 129–30, 134
Adjustment, 193, 206. *See also* Tampering
Administrators, responsibilities of, 91, 99, 227. *See also* Principals
Adults, motivation of, 27–28
Aims
 cause-and-effect diagram and, 159
 for classroom improvement, 69, 133
 for district improvement, 101
 for education law, 209, 210
 in fourth generation management, 227
 importance of, 3–4
 for maintaining enthusiasm, 115
 measuring information and, 37, 38
 measuring knowledge and, 55, 63
 in PDSA cycle, 133
 for school improvement, 91, 100
 for student improvement, 87
 as system elements, 3, 19, 209, 210
Analytic scoring guides, 59, 235–37
Annual measurements, 65–75
Assessment. *See* Quality measurement
Attitudes, societal. *See* Societal pressures
Attitudes, surveys of, 112–14, 180
Authority, as power, 33
Automobile metaphor, 3
Averages
 in control chart, 189
 grade level and, 50–51

B

Barriers between subsystems, 221
Behavior, school standards for, 92
Best efforts, 160
Binomial distribution, 191
Blaming, xxi–xxii, 21
 control charts and, 185, 189
Bones, of fishbone diagrams, 159–60

C

California Learning Assessment System, 214
Cause-and-effect diagrams, 159–64
Causes, 159. *See also* Common causes; Root causes; Special causes
c (count) charts, 186, 188–89
Central line, 189
Change
 avoidance of, 217
 compared to improvement, xxi, 5–7, 147
 leadership for, xvi, 220–21
 pendulum of, 24
 responsibility for, xvi, 48
 time period for, 69, 72–73
Charter schools, 19
Children, motivation of, 27–29, 111. *See also* Enthusiasm; Students
Classroom improvement. *See also* Quality measurement
 measurement of, 65–75
 steps for, 133–34
Class run charts. *See* Run charts, class
Class scatter diagrams. *See* Scatter diagrams
Class size, and reading scores, 177
Common causes, 185–99, 206
Comparisons. *See also* Correlations
 of enthusiasm, by gender, 127
 of enthusiasm, by grade level and subject, 117–26
 of SAT scores, 136–51
 of students, 85, 87, 88–90
Competition
 motivation and, 27
 ranking and, 147
 status quo and, 219
Comprehensive Test of Basic Skills (CTBS), 170–72
Conservative, as a label, 24
Constancy of purpose, 220
Continual improvement, 94, 97, 147
Continuum of quality, scales for, 55–63

243